Managing Editor
Mara Ellen Guckian

Editor in Chief
Karen J. Goldfluss, M.S. Ed.

Creative Director
Sarah M. Fournier

Cover Artist
Diem Pascarella

Illustrator
Kelly McMahon

Art Coordinator
Renée Mc Elwee

Imaging
Amanda R. Harter

Publisher
Mary D. Smith, M.S. Ed.

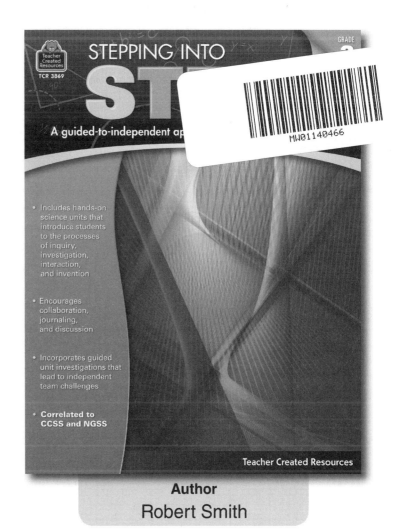

STEPPING INTO STEM

A guided-to-independent approach

- Includes hands-on science units that introduce students to the processes of inquiry, investigation, interaction, and invention

- Encourages collaboration, journaling, and discussion

- Incorporates guided unit investigations that lead to independent team challenges

- Correlated to CCSS and NGSS

Teacher Created Resources

Author
Robert Smith

CORRELATED TO CCSS & NGSS

For correlations to the Common Core State Standards, see page 159 of this book or visit *http://www.teachercreated.com/standards/*. For correlations to the Next Generation Science Standards, see page 160.

Teacher Created Resources

12621 Western Avenue
Garden Grove, CA 92841
www.teachercreated.com
ISBN: 978-1-4206-3869-1

©2016 Teacher Created Resources
Reprinted, 2017

Made in U.S.A.

Teacher Created Resources

C O N T E N T S

Introduction

PROJECT-BASED LEARNING

As educators, we are being required to place more emphasis on science, technology, engineering, and math (STEM) to ensure that today's students will be prepared for their future careers. Additionally, it is important that children learn and practice the 21st-century skills of collaboration, critical thinking, problem solving, and digital literacy in their daily curricula. It is imperative that students learn these collaborative skills, but acquiring these skills is not without challenge. *Stepping into STEM* provides students with needed practice in these areas.

Project-based learning, simply put, is learning by doing. Project-based learning, or PBL, tends to be deeper learning that is more relevant to students, and thus remembered longer. We need to educate students to be global competitors, and to do so, we must help them to think creatively, take risks, and put what they are learning into practice. After all, it doesn't do much good to know a formula if you don't know when to use it. Students also need to learn the value of failure as a learning experience. Some of the ideas and efforts they make during an activity will not work. This can turn into a very positive experience since knowing what won't work (and why) can possibly lead to the discovery of what will work!

Reading informational material provides needed background, but *doing* makes the difference. Concepts, ideas, and experiences of hands-on activities remain lodged in the brain for retrieval when needed.

In STEM curriculum, project-based learning is a must! Its collaborative style guarantees that 21st-century skills are fully integrated into the curriculum while supporting students' academic and socio-emotional growth. Furthermore, PBL allows teachers to immediately assess what students comprehend and to adapt curriculum accordingly.

CONNECTING SCIENCE, TECHNOLOGY, ENGINEERING, AND MATH

STEM activities blend science and engineering learning experiences. Technology—both simple and high-tech—provides the framework for recording information. Phones, tablets, and computers are effective in recording and comparing activity results. The math element might involve sequencing, patterns, or recognizing shapes, size, and volume. Comparisons are expressed in decimals, fractions, ratios, and percentages, as well as measurements, graphs, charts, and other visual representations.

THE NEED FOR INTERACTION AND COLLABORATION

Today's scientists and engineers share ideas, experiments, and solutions—as well as failures—with colleagues around the globe. Student scientists and engineers, like their professional counterparts, need experience working with partners while in a collaborative and supportive environment. They need to exchange ideas, test theories, perform experiments, modify their experiments, try novel approaches (even those that may not appear useful or serious), and cooperate with each other in all aspects of the project as they seek to accomplish their objective.

Successful teams are able to work together and to be respectful even when they disagree. Each team member must also be responsible and accountable for his or her part of the work. Depending upon the activity, students may use the Design Process or the Scientific Method in order to accomplish their objectives.

A basic requirement of these collaborative efforts is a willingness to seriously consider all suggestions from the members of the team. Ideas should be considered, tried, tested, and compared for use in the project. Students should work together to select the most efficient and practical ideas, then methodically test each one for its useful application in the activity.

THE DESIGN PROCESS

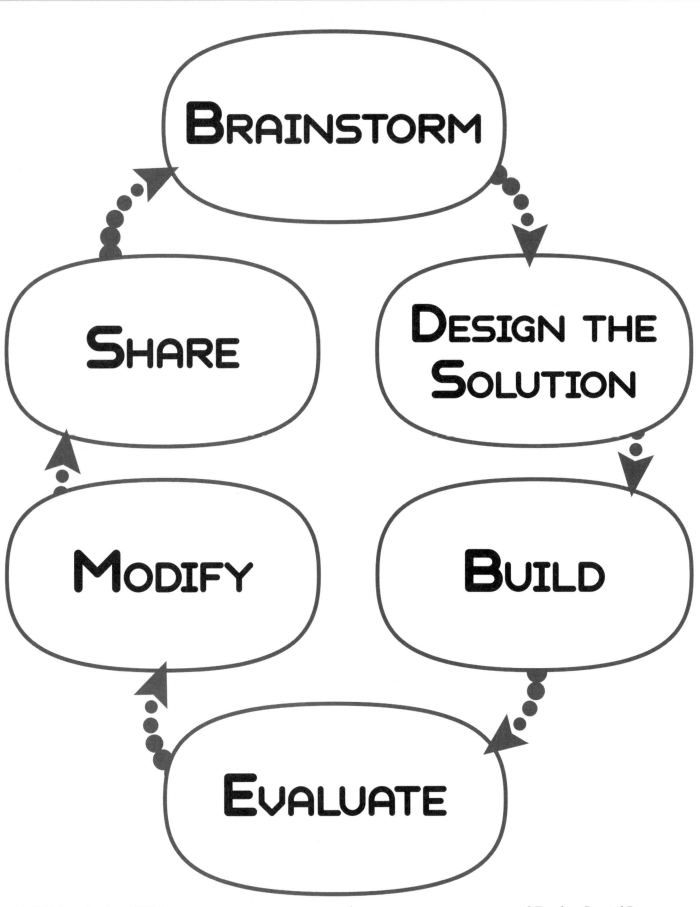

THE DESIGN PROCESS WORKSHEET

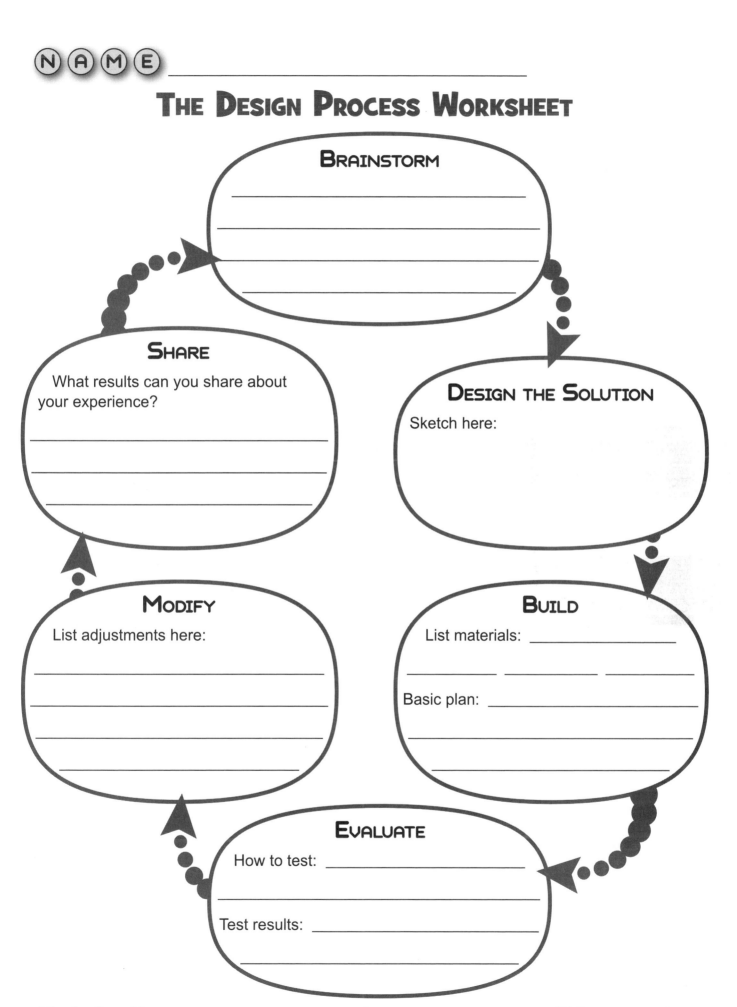

BRAINSTORM

_____

_____

_____

_____

SHARE

What results can you share about your experience?

_____

_____

_____

DESIGN THE SOLUTION

Sketch here:

MODIFY

List adjustments here:

_____

_____

_____

_____

BUILD

List materials: _____

_____ _____ _____

Basic plan: _____

_____

_____

EVALUATE

How to test: _____

_____

Test results: _____

_____

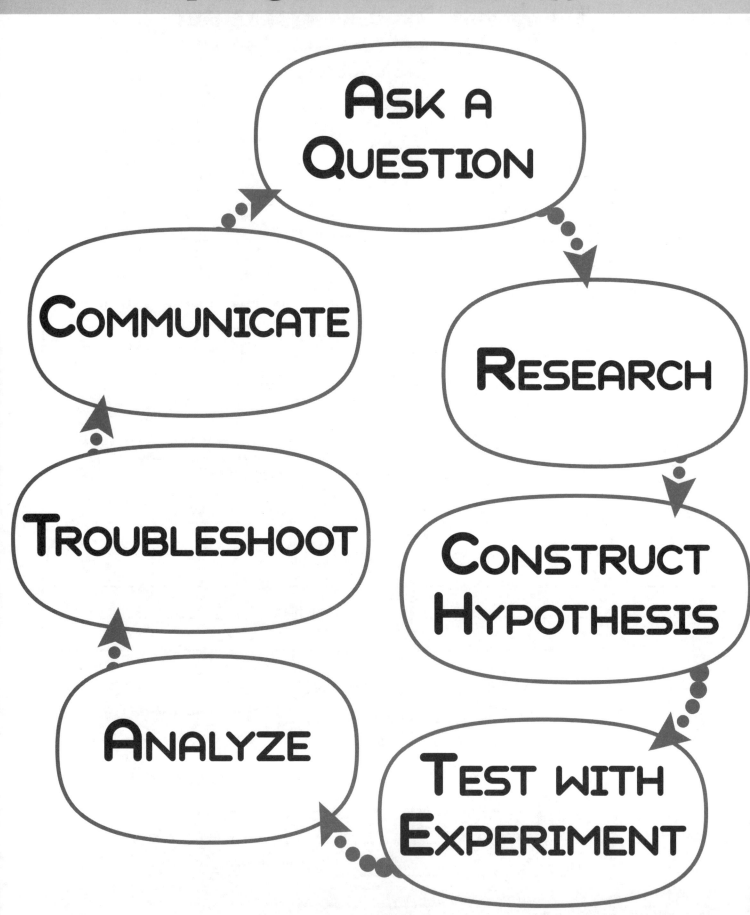

THE SCIENTIFIC METHOD WORKSHEET

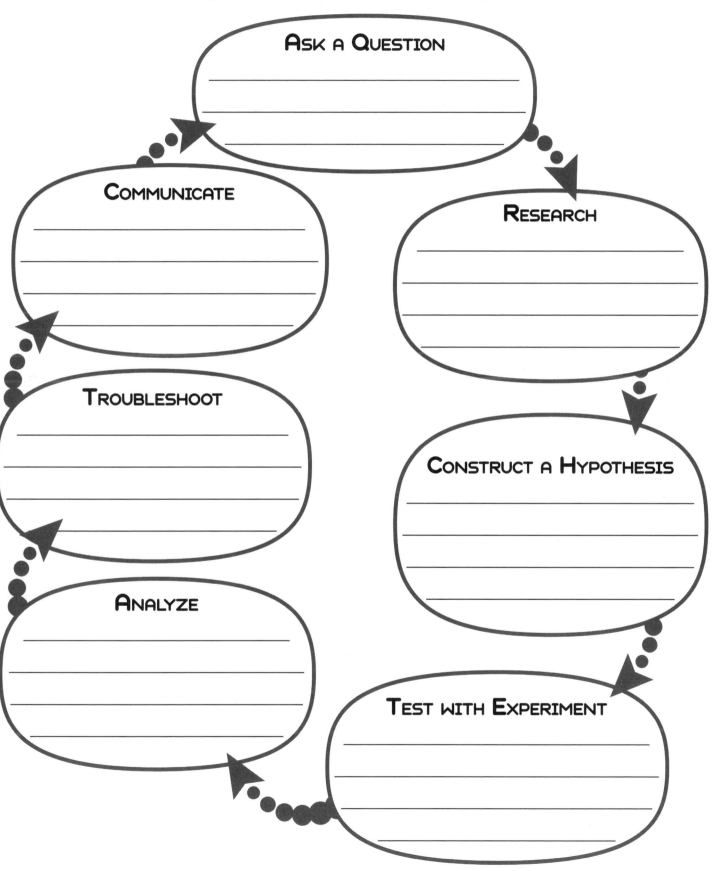

ASK A QUESTION

COMMUNICATE

RESEARCH

TROUBLESHOOT

CONSTRUCT A HYPOTHESIS

ANALYZE

TEST WITH EXPERIMENT

GROWING CRITICAL THINKERS

While all members of a team need to be respected and heard, members of the team also need to critically examine each idea to see if it is feasible. This is part of both the design process used by engineers and the scientific method employed by scientists.

Students need to apply their learned experiences in these activities, and serious attention should be given to testing each idea for feasibility and practicality. Students can develop this skill by considering each serious suggestion, testing it for workability, and then determining its value. In order to accomplish this task, students need to examine the available materials, work with them in an organized way, record their results, and compare these results.

Critical thinkers are organized and methodical in their testing and experimentation. They examine the ideas generated in the free flow of comments and discussions. They determine which ideas can be tested and then carefully compared for useful application to the problem. They keep open minds. Critical thinkers base their judgments on observations and proven outcomes. Critical thinkers aren't negative, but they are skeptical until they observe the results of an activity.

"Show me."   "Let's check it out."

"How can we test it to see if it works?"

One of the hallmarks of a scientist is the inclination to ask questions. Another is making the effort to seek answers through effective investigations, tests, and experiments. You want to encourage your student scientists to practice critical thinking by asking thoughtful questions that use academic vocabulary and by developing creative ways to test possible solutions.

THE 4 IS: INQUIRE • INVESTIGATE • INTERACT • INVENT

The four basic elements of an effective science or STEM activity can be categorized as Inquiry, Investigation, Interaction, and Invention.

1. INQUIRY is the process of determining what you wish to learn about a scientific or natural phenomenon. The natural phenomenon can be as simple as a student's swing moving back and forth, a schoolyard game of marbles, or sucking on a straw. Some of the same principles of science may apply to a helicopter rescue of a swimmer, a batted ball in a major-league game, or the process of getting water out of a ditch. The questions are always the same:

"Why did it happen? Will it happen every time? What happens if … you change the length of the swing, the size of the marble, the diameter of the straw, the weight of the swimmer, the diameter of the ball, or the length of the siphon hose in the ditch?"

In the simplest form, to **Inquire** is to question: Why . . . ?, What if . . . ?, How . . . ?

2. INVESTIGATION is the action a scientist takes to learn more about the question. It involves the process a student scientist needs to follow. The investigation can involve background research, the process of doing an experiment, and interpreting the results. Reading a science text about the workings of the pendulum is not the same as actually constructing a working pendulum, adjusting it to different lengths and weights, and carefully observing its features and behaviors in varying circumstances. Measuring these things in mathematical terms provides the opportunity for valid comparisons as well.

3. INTERACTION requires student scientists to collaborate with one or more classmates. Together they assess the problem or question, determine and carry out an investigation, and analyze the results.

From a practical point of view, experiments done with students are more effective with teams of two. In larger groups, one or more team members often feel left out, don't get to actually do the hands-on construction, and can end up engaging in distracting behaviors. Teams of two require the active involvement of both individuals in all phases of the activity, all the time. The one off-task student in a team can be refocused by a partner or the teacher.

It is important to have enough materials and equipment for each team's basic activity. The materials used in the activities in this book are inexpensive and easily available to facilitate two-person teams.

4. INVENTION is the final stage of the 4 *I*s in a science activity, *i.e.*, the effort to create or invent a solution, modification, or improvement. This can be the most challenging aspect of the activity. At first, suggestions tend to be far out, impractical, silly, or impossible to realize with the available materials. The most effective teams discuss possible solutions and then start manipulating the materials as a form of "thinking with their hands."

The invention aspect of the activity is nearly always the final step of the activity. For instance, after multiple sessions manipulating and measuring results with a pendulum, students should have enough background and hands-on experience to invent an application for this tool. It may be a toy swing for a doll, a time-keeping mechanism for a class activity, such as a timed math-facts sheet, or an attempt to make a perpetual motion machine (or one that just lasts longer than anybody else's).

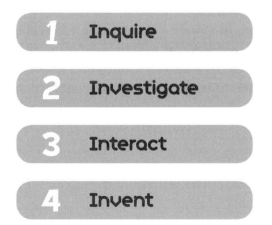

THE NEED FOR JOURNALING

Scientists keep records. They are meticulous in recording the results of their investigations and often refer back to investigations done in previous months and years. They use this information as needed for further investigations, related experiments, and in publishing their work.

Ideally, all students should keep journals recording the investigations on which they have been working. With continued practice, students will develop the habit of journaling after each period of investigation. It is easier for students to keep information in one place and to refer back to previous investigations for discussion and record-keeping purposes. Consider having students use 3-ring binders to keep unit pages together with additional notes, ideas, and sketches.

It is suggested that a separate entry be made for each investigation session. Have students enter the date and investigation title for each new entry. Include a key question for each activity. This is the starting point for each investigation. As students proceed, they should record, using adequate details, the process and materials used to investigate the question. Encourage students to use appropriate vocabulary when journaling.

The variations in technique, the engineering adjustments, the technology employed, and the results of each modification should be recorded. The mathematical applications should also be noted. If the length of the fishing line was doubled or cut in half, this is critical information. If the weight was doubled from 8 grams to 16 grams, it should be noted, and then the effect of the changes should be recorded for each subsequent trial.

The most important information in the journal should be the research team's conclusions about the testable questions the team was investigating. Individual researchers may draw separate conclusions about these questions, but the conclusions need to be based on objective facts and recorded information.

THE REVIEW DISCUSSIONS

The journal entries should also be the "notes" student scientists use when sharing their information during each class review discussion. Either the *Design Process* or the *Scientific Method* can be used, depending on the topic. The teacher can act as the moderator of each discussion and should ensure that each student gets an opportunity to share his or her experiences, results, and scientific observations. These discussions work well as 10-minute closure activities at the end of each activity period.

Encourage all students to take turns sharing the results of their activities and the conclusions they drew from their experiments. Data summaries may include photos, videos, or other relevant materials.

Model and encourage serious reporting. Encourage students to incorporate the new vocabulary into their discussions, their journaling, and their presentation pieces.

The writing (journaling) and the review are vital elements in the design process. They provide students with the opportunity to share their experiences, and they serve as an excellent part of the assessment process. It is suggested that you allow at least 20 minutes to complete these activities.

You may choose to act as moderator. You can allow students to share, as teams or as individuals, about each activity and other activities they have done on related subjects. You may also use smaller groups with student moderators.

KEEPING THINGS IN PERSPECTIVE!

A STEM class will rarely be perfectly quiet! In fact, the low buzz of purposeful conversation is an indicator that students are actively engaged. The teacher serves as the facilitator, providing guidance, crucial information, and directions at the outset. It is important to regularly check on each group to offer encouragement, advice, correction, and support.

Teachers need to evaluate how students are doing as teams proceed with investigations. In addition to guiding the learning process, it is also very important to draw closure on the activity by moderating the final portion of the *Design Process Review* in which you draw conclusions and highlight the core learning concepts embedded in the activity.

Unsuccessful periods happen in any kind of class, no matter how capable the instructor or how gifted the class. Myriad things can go wrong—announcements from the intercom can break the flow of instruction, an activity goes awry, or one of the countless other distractions of school life can occur. You may get a true scientific discussion going but have it go off into areas unrelated to the thrust of the investigation.

But there are also those times when you encounter the pleasant experience of no one paying any attention to the distraction. A visitor or principal enters the room, observes the activity for a moment, and either leaves or joins a group. The science discussion reverts to the main idea and goes smoothly or vigorously along, driven by students who are focused and on task. Yes, it happens!

Students can really "get into" science. They enjoy the openness involved in the activity, the collegial nature of working on a project, the materials they get to manipulate, and the mental stimulation of solving a problem or creating a better product. A good, productive, stimulating science period can make their day—and yours, too.

How to Use This Book

Stepping into STEM is arranged with flexibility in mind. One method is to move from lesson to lesson in each unit and to proceed through the units in order. However, the number and order of units completed throughout the year is completely dependent on classroom and curriculum needs. You may want to choose the activities you are more familiar with or those which fit your school schedule better. The organization of each unit moves from teacher-directed activities, to more student-driven activities, to a final challenge activity which allows students to create their own unique products or inventions. Students should be encouraged to follow the Design Process while doing the activities in each unit.

PACING UNITS AND LESSONS

The amount of time allotted for completion of each unit can vary. You may choose to utilize some or all of the units and can intersperse them througout the year, building each unit into your science curriculum. If a unit topic fits in well with what is currently being taught, embed it into the schedule where possible. Since these unit investigations were developed to foster a STEM approach to learning, they do not have to be tied to any specific time frame or subject in the science curriculum.

To get the most out of a unit, it is suggested that a few sessions be allotted in order to complete the activities. These can be spread out as needed. Usually, an activity can be done in about an hour. For those fortunate enough to have a one-and-a-half hour period, students will have more time to explore the variations in each project and to extend their creative explorations. Remember that the unit activities can be broken into more than one session! Be sure to allow focused time for journaling and recording information in each period.

VOCABULARY AND DISCUSSIONS

Share and discuss the STEM Vocabulary List (page 17) and the unit vocabulary lists with students. Identify and use the terms frequently throughout the sessions in order to reinforce essential subject-area vocabulary. Enlarge each unit list in order to create posters for student reference or photocopy a list for each student to keep in his or her journaling notebook.

Encourage discussions within groups and between groups as long as the discussions are focused on the topic. At the end of each activity, allow time for teacher- or student-moderated review activities, in which individuals share their experiments, designs, results, and conclusions based on their research.

A general activity period could allow 5 to 7 minutes for teacher introduction and review of previous learning, 5 minutes to efficiently distribute supplies, and 30 to 40 minutes to complete the activity involving science, technology, engineering, and math. The remaining time should be devoted to science journaling.

TEACHER AND STUDENT RUBRICS

Use the teacher rubric on page 18 to evaluate team progress, time-on-task, and student interaction, and to reinforce STEM objectives. Students who are focused on the objective and methodically trying different ways to solve a problem are doing science. So are those who are responding a bit randomly to their own ideas and trying them out.

As student groups work through each investigation, they should complete the student rubric on page 19 in order to reinforce the processes they have used and to reflect on the procedures they have followed.

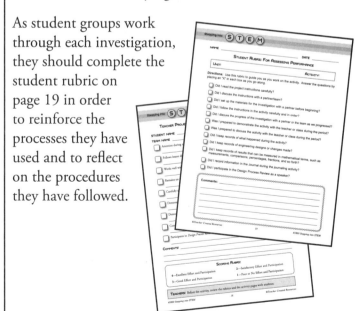

NOTE: Explain both rubrics to students before starting the units. It is important for them to know how their work will be evaluated and what steps they should follow as they work on a unit investigation.

CHALLENGE ACTIVITY

Each of the units culminates in a challenge assignment. Students are asked to create a new version of a product or to extend experimentation based on the activities in the unit. Students are advised to look over their journals and other documentation collected during the unit and to pick an extension. They are to use either the Design Process to create something new, or the Scientific Method, in which nature and how it works is the focus. The choice of method used will be determined by the objective of the assignment and whether engineering or science will be the focus. Opportunities for both are provided in this book.

For example, students doing the Boats and Barges unit make clay boats first and later, foil rafts. They observe which vessels carry the biggest and most balanced loads. They learn the advantages of different materials—the limitations of foil or clay, for example—and the advantages of spreading a load over a wider area. Students then use the Design Process as a guide for the challenge assignment to design and build their own floating vessels using materials from the unit.

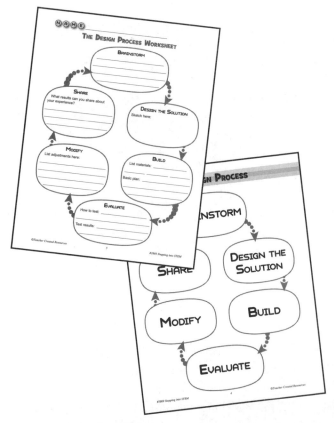

The Scientific Method is used when students approach a culminating challenge activity with more emphasis on science—as they do in the unit on Solutions, Mixtures, and Emulsions. Here, the emphasis is not on building (engineering) but on testing a hypothesis about ingredients and what might happen when they are mixed.

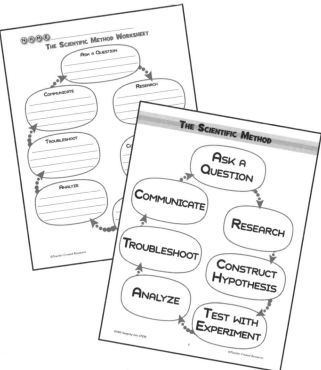

Allow time for imagination, frustration, and revamping during the building and testing periods of the challenge assignments. Use the grading rubric to evaluate creativity, success, effort, and on-task work time.

TEAM MANAGEMENT

The activities in this series were designed to maximize student participation. Students will work in pairs or small collaborative teams. The collaborative process is essential to construct the apparatus and create the models. Four hands and two minds working together are more efficient and effective than individuals proceeding alone.

Lesson Notes for the Teacher

LESSON 1—GUIDED ACTIVITY

The first lesson is designed so that the teacher can guide and control the pace of the activity and can ensure that students know how to function in this type of science activity and with these materials. It is more teacher-directed in terms of time and following specific directions than later lessons in the unit.

Providing guidance through the beginning phases of each unit will set the stage for student groups to continue with their investigations and discussions throughout the units. This is also an opportunity for the teacher to note which teams or students might be struggling and to provide more assistance to them.

LESSONS—YOUR TURN

Review students' findings and ideas related to their investigations in Activity 1. Discuss how students will be exploring how a project works under various conditions. This can be an independent collaborative group activity or students can work in pairs.

The next two or three lessons allow students to work at their own pace as they do the activities. The teacher circulates through the room, giving advice, encouragement, and correction as needed. Students work in pairs.

FINAL LESSON—THE CHALLENGE

The final lesson in each unit involves a Challenge Activity in which students apply what they have learned in earlier lessons in order to solve a specific problem or to make the fastest, best, or most unique application of the concepts learned. Students should work in pairs.

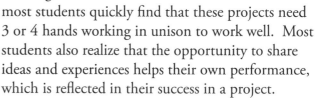

ABOUT TEAMS

Although there are always students who prefer to work alone— and have difficulty working with others— most students quickly find that these projects need 3 or 4 hands working in unison to work well. Most students also realize that the opportunity to share ideas and experiences helps their own performance, which is reflected in their success in a project.

You may want to have students switch partners when you start a new unit or after partners have been together for a few units.

Whenever possible, keep the teams small (two people) and therefore more likely to keep their hands and minds occupied and on task.

The activities in this series are designed for full participation by all students with all students actively engaged at all times. All students will use the materials and should have access to the necessary equipment. Students work in collaborative teams in order to facilitate learning, but all students are actively engaged with all aspects of the projects.

There are very few lone scientists working in private anymore in this age of scientific and technological discovery. Teamwork matters—kinesthetic experiences and collaborative interaction with peers are essential aspects of science instruction.

EL Tips

Review vocabulary with EL students to assure understanding. Ask EL students to describe the intent and focus of the project. Pair EL students with EO (English Only) students when needed. Strongly encourage the journaling aspect of the activities, use of the Scientific Method and/or the Design Process Reviews.

A Note About Materials

Many materials used in these projects are easy to find and, in most cases, are reusable. Some are school supplies. Virtually all of the materials used in this series are available at relatively inexpensive cost in local stores—especially wholesale places and some dollar discount stores. A few are available in local hardware stores. There should be a sufficient supply of materials for each team.

Refer to individual units for the listings of specific materials. Be sure to collect all materials ahead of time, and consider ways to distribute, use, and store materials prior to introducing each new unit. If possible, establish an area in the classroom where materials can be accessed easily.

14

Addressing Standards

NEXT GENERATION SCIENCE STANDARDS

The National Research Council of the National Academy of Sciences published "A Framework for K–12 Science Education: Practices, Crosscutting Concepts, and Core Ideas" (NRC, 2012).

Its purpose was to serve as a guide for the 26 states presently collaborating to develop the Next Generation Science Standards. The framework defined science "to mean the traditional natural sciences: physics, chemistry, biology, and (more recently) earth, space, and environmental sciences."

The council used the term engineering "to mean any engagement in a systematic practice of design to achieve solutions to particular human problems."

They used the term "technology" to include all types of human-made systems and processes—not simply modern computational and communications devices. Technologies result when engineers apply their understanding of the natural world and human behavior to design ways that satisfy human needs and wants.

One of the critical elements of the Next Generation Science Standards is the effort to develop students' competence in science practices. These are the behaviors that scientists actually engage in as they conduct their investigations. When students or scientists engage in science, they are deeply involved in inquiry as they use a range of skills and knowledge at the same time.

The engineering practices "are the behaviors that engineers engage in as they apply science and math to design solutions to problems." Engineering design has similarities to scientific inquiry. However, there are differences in the two subjects.

Engineering design involves creating a question that can be solved through design:

"How can I make a clay boat that holds more weight?"

"What happens when I add other materials to the boat?"

Scientific inquiry involves creating a question that can be solved through investigation, such as, "What happens to a solution when you add alcohol to it?" Try to ask "what" questions instead of "why" questions; they are open-ended and focus on what can be observed during experimentation.

Engineering questions may produce scientific information. Strengthening the engineering component in these standards helps students recognize the interrelationship between the four cornerstones of STEM instruction: Science, Technology, Engineering, and Math.

The **Disciplinary Core Ideas (DCI)** in the Next Generation Science Standards are broad, essential ideas in science instruction that span across several grade levels and areas of science instruction, including the life sciences, earth and space science, physical sciences, engineering, and technology.

Cross-cutting Concepts are ideas that bridge the boundaries between science and engineering, as well as helping students to connect different ideas in the sciences. They provide students with an organizational framework for connecting science and engineering concepts into coherent patterns.

The 7 Cross-cutting Concepts
1. Patterns
2. Cause and Effect
3. Scale, Proportion, and Quantity
4. Systems and System Models
5. Energy and Matter
6. Structure and Function
7. Stability and Change

Most good science activities exhibit examples of several of these concepts, of course, and students should begin to notice these concepts as they do the experiments in this book. Their journals should specify one or more of these concepts each time they write about a project.

Addressing Standards *(cont.)*

COMMON CORE STATE STANDARDS

The math applications required for conducting complete, detailed science activities are as essential as the apparatus and materials used in the activities. An emphasis on math and reading literacy is built into the Common Core as a prominent aspect of the nearly national consensus that Common Core provides. The application of both skills is essential to STEM education.

Teachers may find that they need to explain the application of a wide variety of math concepts as they arise in STEM activities. These math activities may involve measurement, computing percentages, working with fractions and mixed numbers, measuring and converting units of time, measuring and comparing distances, working with metric units, and many others. Students often know the processes in these math concepts but have no idea how to use them in real-life or science applications.

The Common Core State Standards have placed a strong emphasis on math applications—not just the mechanics of a skill. Utilizing math in comparing various results in a science activity will increase understanding of many concepts. Metric measurement—the common system used in science—becomes second nature to students who routinely use it to measure and compare distance, volume, and capacity, for example. Percentages, ratios, and other comparative measurements have more meaning when applied to hands-on activities.

The Common Core Standards likewise are focused on informational reading in science (as well as social studies). Students need to become familiar with sources beyond the textbook in order to research science information. These involve both paper and digital sources.

The writing standards of the Common Core also expect students to routinely write effectively on science topics. The activities in this book provide guided opportunities to take notes and to write brief reports on each activity while including all relevant details.

Common Core State Standards emphasize the development of speaking and listening skills, and encourage discussion and collaboration. *Stepping into STEM* provides opportunities for students to share their collective writings with each other in *The Design Process Review* or the *Scientific Process Review*.

STANDARDS CORRELATIONS

Correlations for both the Common Core State Standards and the Next Generation Science Standards are provided for the units in this book.

General standards correlations for each unit can be found on pages 159–160. You can also visit *www.teachercreated.com/standards* for more comprehensive correlations charts.

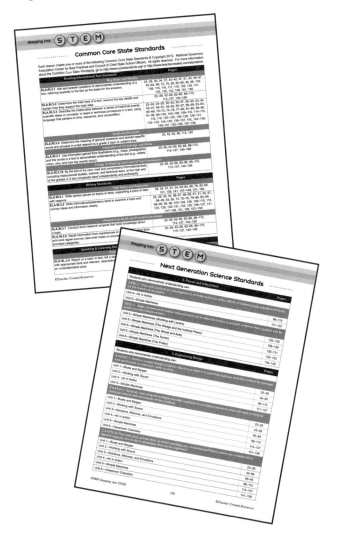

STEM VOCABULARY

The following vocabulary words are used in STEM explorations. Discuss these terms and use them often during the activities and in your journal.

brainstorm—a method of problem solving in which all members of a group spontaneously discuss ideas

collaborate—to work with one or more peers in a team to assess the problem or question, determine the nature of the investigation, and analyze results

communicate—to talk with others

data—facts, information in number form, and observations collected to be analyzed

design—an outline or plan

Design Process—a series of steps used by engineers to create products and/or processes

efficient—working well without unusual effort

evaluate—to make a judgment

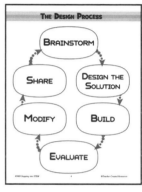

hypothesis—a prediction that can be tested; a serious scientific guess or idea that works as a starting point for further investigation

innovation—an improvement of an existing product, system, or way of doing something

inquiry—the process of determining what you wish to learn about a scientific or natural phenomenon

invent—the effort to design a solution, modification, or improvement

investigate—the action a scientist takes to learn more about the question

manipulate—to control or change something, often with the hands

modify—to change or adjust

observation—scientific information gathered during an experiment

reaction—a chemical change

Scientific Method—a series of steps used by scientists in order to carry out experiments

unique—special or different; unusual; one of a kind

variable—something that can be changed

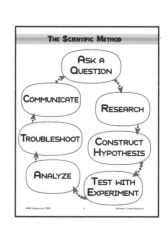

Teacher Rubric for Assessing Student Performance

STUDENT NAME _____ **DATE** _____

TEAM NAME _____

☐ Pays attention during teacher instruction: _____

_____

☐ Follows lesson directions: _____

_____

☐ Works well with the team: _____

_____

☐ Remains on task during the period: _____

_____

☐ Carefully records information, trials, etc. during the investigation: _____

_____

☐ Demonstrates creativity in problem solving: _____

_____

☐ Demonstrates persistence in problem solving: _____

_____

☐ Completes journaling entries: _____

_____

☐ Participates in *Design Process Review*: _____

_____

COMMENTS: _____

_____

_____

Scoring Rubric

4—Excellent Effort and Participation **2**—Satisfactory Effort and Participation

3—Good Effort and Participation **1**—Poor or No Effort and Participation

TEACHERS: Before the activity, review the rubrics and the activity pages with students.

NAME _____ DATE _____

Student Rubric for Assessing Performance

Unit:	Activity:

Directions: Use this rubric to guide you as you work on the activity. Answer the questions by placing an "X" in each box as you go along.

☐ Did I read the project instructions carefully?

☐ Did I discuss the instructions with a partner/team?

☐ Did I set up the materials for the investigation with a partner before beginning?

☐ Did I follow the instructions in the activity carefully and in order?

☐ Did I discuss how our investigation was going with my partner or the team as we progressed?

☐ Was I prepared to demonstrate the activity to the teacher or class during the period?

☐ Was I prepared to discuss the activity with the teacher or class during the period?

☐ Did I keep records of what happened during the activity?

☐ Did I keep records of engineering designs or changes made?

☐ Did I keep records of results that can be measured in mathematical terms, such as measurements, comparisons, percentages, fractions, and so forth?

☐ Did I record information in my journal during the journaling activity?

☐ Did I participate in the Design Process Review as a speaker?

Comments: _____
_____
_____
_____
_____
_____

BOATS AND BARGES

4 sessions: 1 session for each activity (approximately 1 to 1½ hours per session)

Focus: Physical Science—buoyancy, flotation

CONNECTIONS AND SUGGESTIONS

SCIENCE—Students will be exploring Archimedes' Principle and constructing boats capable of carrying cargo (pennies). Clay, aluminum foil, Styrofoam, and plastic frozen food containers are used in the four activities in this unit. These durable materials work well with the surface tension of water to support the flotation devices in these activities.

Modeling clay is denser than water and would ordinarily sink. In the activities in this unit, students will reshape a clay ball into forms that will float. Clay is lighter than water when spread out over a wide enough area. It is generally waterproof and reusable as well. As a result, modeling clay is especially useful for buoyancy and flotation experiments. (Try to purchase clay in one-pound boxes.)

Note: "Play-doh-type" clay does not work because it disintegrates in water.

TECHNOLOGY APPLICATIONS—Students can use computers or personal tablets to do research on displacement, buoyancy, and Archimedes' Principle. Additionally, they can photograph or record their observations and responses as they create boats, rafts, and other floating vessels. They might also use computer software to record the problems encountered, the solutions attempted, the success rate of each activity, different approaches used, and suggestions for improvement.

ENGINEERING—Students will work using the design process to build vessels and to determine which designs will support the most weight without sinking. Students will be able to explain why some boat designs work better than others.

MATH—The measurement applications in this unit require students to record the precise number of pennies used and to compute the pennies' weights. (**Note:** Pennies made from 1982 onward weigh 2.5 grams. Those produced before 1982 are mostly 3.11 grams. Use the more common weight of pennies from the last 30+ years.)

DISCUSSION PROMPT: What is Archimedes' Principle?

Archimedes was a Greek scientist who lived long ago. He made his discovery while taking a bath! He discovered that an object placed in water would float if the displaced water weighed more than the object doing the displacing. For instance, if a 12-pound bowling ball is placed in water, it will sink because it only displaces 10 pounds of water. A balloon that is the same size as the bowling ball will float because it weighs less and displaces (or moves) less water.

BOATS AND BARGES

UNIT MATERIALS (for a class of 30 to 35)

- ☐ aluminum foil
- ☐ baby lotion (optional)
- ☐ balloons
- ☐ craft sticks
- ☐ dental floss or knife
- ☐ heavy item (bowling ball or brick)
- ☐ modeling clay ($2\frac{1}{2}$ lbs)
- ☐ pennies ($10.00)
- ☐ plastic, frozen-food trays
- ☐ round toothpicks
- ☐ rubber cement
- ☐ rulers
- ☐ scales
- ☐ straws
- ☐ Styrofoam trays or boxes
- ☐ water
- ☐ water tubs, dishpans, or bussing trays (at least 3 inches deep)

NOTES

_____

_____

_____

_____

_____

_____

_____

_____

_____

_____

_____

_____

_____

_____

FIND OUT MORE

Float or Sink: Why do things float? Why do things sink?—Lesson for Kids

https://www.youtube.com/watch?v=c8kszaZGLKE

NOVA Online: Bouyancy Basics

https://www.pbs.org/wgbh/nova/lasalle/buoybasics.html

Science Videos for Kids Grades 1–7

https://www.makemegenius.com

Safety Note: All websites should be checked prior to student viewing to be certain that content is appropriate.

BOATS AND BARGES VOCABULARY

barge—a flat-bottomed boat for carrying freight

buoyant—able to float because of weight, density, and/or shape

collapse—to fall down or cave in

density—the quality or state of being dense; the amount of mass an object has compared to its volume or size (anything that has less density than water will float)

diffusion—the spreading out of molecules within a solution

displacement—being pushed out of place; if the weight of the water displaced (10 lbs.) is less than the weight of the item (12-lb. bowling ball) in the water, the item will sink.

float—to rest on top of a liquid

pliable—easily bent, folded, or twisted

raft—a flat, floating structure

sculpt—to carefully construct by hand

sink—to fall below the surface of a liquid

surface area—the part of an object that is exposed to the surface of the water

surface tension—the "sticking together" of the molecules on the surface of a liquid allows it to behave like an elastic skin; for example, the surface of water allows heavier objects to float on it.

trial—a test of performance or other qualities

vessel—a ship or large boat; a hollow container

EXPLANATION FOR BOUYANCY

Bouyancy is the upward force on an object produced by the surrounding liquid (or gas).

When an object is placed in water, it pushes some of the water out of the way. It displaces water.

- The object will float if it weighs less than the water that is pushed out of the way.
- The object will sink if it weighs more than the water pushed out of the way.

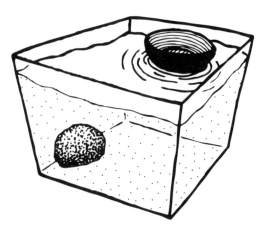

BOATS AND BARGES

DISPLACEMENT

Did you ever wonder *why* some things sink and other things float? How can a huge tanker ship float if a small rock sinks? It doesn't seem to make sense, does it? There must be more to the problem than just weight.

It has to do with how much water moves when you put the object in the water. The scientific word for this is **displacement**. The water gets "displaced," or moved, when an object is put in it. If the object weighs more than the amount of water that it moves, that object will sink.

Do you float when you take a bath? No, you do not! You can see the level of the water go up if you watch the side of the tub when you sit down. The water level rises because you are displacing, or moving, the water. The amount of water you "displace" in the tub weighs less than you do.

If you lay on the water in a pool, you can float, but if you sit on the steps of a pool, you do not float, right? This is because when you sit in the pool, you take up more room and move more water out of the way. You **displace** more water! When you try to lay flat on the water in a pool, you don't displace as much water, so you float.

BOATS AND BARGES

ARCHIMEDES—SCIENTIST, MATHEMATICIAN, INVENTOR

Archimedes (Are-kim-e-dees) lived in Greece long ago. He solved problems. He figured out why some things float and others sink. His discovery is now called *Archimedes' Principle*. People say he figured it out one day while taking a bath!

TESTING ARCHIMEDES' PRINCIPLE

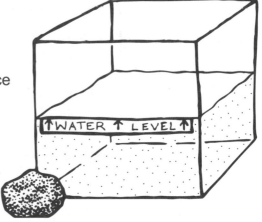

1. Fill a container halfway with water.

2. Mark the level of water in the container with a piece of tape.

3. Make a ball using one ounce of clay and place it in the water. Does it sink? It should.

4. Now, flatten out that ball of clay and try again. It should float and it will take up less space in the water!

How would you explain *displacement*? Can you illustrate displacement?

_____

_____

_____

_____

_____

_____

_____

CONSTRUCTING CLAY BOATS

Directions: Work in pairs. Each student should start by making his or her own boat. Use one ounce of modeling clay for each boat. As you work the clay, the body oils from your hands will make the modeling clay easier to manipulate, more likely to float, and better at keeping water out.

TEAM MATERIALS
- dental floss
- modeling clay (1 ounce per student)
- round toothpicks
- water tubs (at least 3" deep)
- pennies
- plastic knives

NOTE: Modeling clay is easily sliced to make segments by using dental floss or a knife.

ROUND OR OVAL CLAY BOAT DESIGN—TRIAL 1

1. The goal of this activity is to make a boat that will float. Work with the clay for a few minutes. Use your hands and fingers to warm up the clay and to make it soft and pliable.

2. Once the clay is soft and easy to use, start creating a boat. Make a round or oval-shaped base with sides.

3. Use a toothpick to help sculpt the design. Sketch your design in the frame.

4. Place the completed boat in the water in order to be tested.

   — If the boat does not float, take it out, remold it, and try again.

   — If the boat does float, place a penny in it. Does it still float?

   YES   NO

5. Keep adding pennies to the floating boat. Add a few at a time until the boat sinks.

6. Record how many pennies the boat held before it sank. Use the sheet on the following page to record your results.

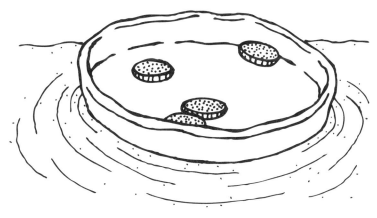

CONSTRUCTING CLAY BOATS

ROUND OR OVAL CLAY BOAT DESIGN—TRIAL 2

1. Remove the boat and the pennies from the water and remake the boat. Sketch your new boat in the frame on the right.

2. Try a different round or oval design or just rework the clay to make a thinner, larger boat.

3. Make notes on the recording sheet below to keep track of the changes you made.

4. Place the boat in the water again. Keep adding pennies carefully until your boat sinks.

5. Use the recording sheet below to record the number of pennies used in each trial until the boats sank.

6. Use a calculator to help you compute the weight of the pennies.

ROUND OR OVAL BOAT TRIALS

Trial	Number of Pennies	Weight (Each penny weighs 2.5 grams.)
1	_____	_____ (_____ × 2.5 = _____)
2	_____	_____ (_____ × 2.5 = _____)

Notes and Observations

_____

_____

_____

_____

CONSTRUCTING CLAY BOATS

SQUARE OR RECTANGULAR BOAT DESIGN—TRIAL 1

1. Rework the clay into a ball. Work it with your hands for a few minutes until it is pliable. This time, remold the clay into a square boat design or a rectangular boat design.

2. Sketch your new design in the frame on the right.

3. Float the new boat to make sure that it is free of holes.

4. Carefully load pennies into the new boat design. Arrange the pennies so that they balance the load. Add pennies carefully until the boat sinks.

5. Use the recording sheet below to record the number of pennies the first square or rectangular boat held before it sank.

SQUARE OR RECTANGULAR BOAT TRIALS		
Trial	Number of Pennies	Weight (Each penny weighs 2.5 grams.)
1	_____	_____ (___ × 2.5 = _____)
2	_____	_____ (___ × 2.5 = _____)
Notes and Observations		

_____

_____

SQUARE OR RECTANGULAR BOAT DESIGN—TRIAL 2

1. Remake your square or rectangular boat. Try to improve your vessel.

2. Sketch or write about the adjustments you make on the second boat in the frame on the right.

3. Float the new boat and test it. Add the pennies slowly.

4. Record the number of pennies in the chart above.

5. Discuss your results.

 NAME _____

CONSTRUCTING CLAY BOATS

TRIANGULAR BOAT DESIGN—TRIAL 1

1. Use clay to make a new boat with a triangular-shaped base. Sketch your boat.
2. Work the clay with hands and fingers to make it pliable.
3. Try using baby lotion or another kind of oil on your hands when working the clay to remove water (from the last trial) and help the clay stick together.
4. Record the results of your triangular boat trials below.

TRIANGULAR BOAT TRIALS

Trial	Number of Pennies	Weight (Each penny weighs 2.5 grams.)
1	_____	_____ (___ × 2.5 = _____)
2	_____	_____ (___ × 2.5 = _____)

Notes and Observations

_____

_____

TRIANGULAR BOAT DESIGN—TRIAL 2

1. Remake your triangular boat. Try to improve your vessel.
2. Sketch or write about the adjustments you make on your triangular boat.
3. Float the new boat and test it.
4. Record the number of pennies in the chart above.
5. Discuss the results of your two tests.

CONSTRUCTING CLAY BOATS

JOURNAL ENTRY

1. Which was the best boat design that you made? _____

   Why? _____

   _____

   _____

2. Which design that you observed was especially interesting? _____
   THINK: What was different about the design?

   _____

   _____

3. Did you use toothpicks, pencils, or other tools to carve your boat?   **YES   NO**

   If so, which tool worked best? _____

   Why? _____

   _____

4. What was the highest number of pennies that your boat carried before it sank? _____

   THINK: Did it matter where you put the pennies and how you arranged them?   **YES   NO**

   Why? _____

   _____

   _____

5. In your opinion, who had the best clay boat? _____

   Why was it so good? _____

   _____

DESIGN PROCESS REVIEW—CONSTRUCTING CLAY BOATS

Directions: Share your observations, journal entries, and other documentation about your experiences constructing vessels with your classmates in a discussion led by your teacher.

 _____

BUILDING BARGES

Directions: Work in pairs. The goal is to build a barge that will be able to carry a load of pennies. Use the materials provided for each team. Two teams can share each tub of water for testing.

TEAM MATERIALS

- 2 craft sticks
- 2 round toothpicks
- 2 three-inch straws
- 3 pieces of 1" square Styrofoam
- 3 pieces of stiff plastic, 1" squares
- modeling clay (1-ounce per student)
- pennies (one roll per student)
- rulers
- water
- water tubs (at least 3" deep)

DESIGNING BARGES—PLANNING

1. Think about the different-shaped clay boats you have already made. Which one seemed to be the sturdiest? _____

2. Which base shape do you think will be better suited to hold the most pennies? Why?

   _____

3. Research different types of barges. Describe what a barge looks like and explain what barges are used for.

   _____

   _____

BARGE 1 DESIGN—TRIAL 1

1. "Think with a pencil" and make a quick design or sketch (below) for a barge you can make from an ounce of clay. You may also use any of the following materials:

   - 2 craft sticks
   - 2 toothpicks
   - 3 pieces of Styrofoam
   - 2 short straws
   - 3 pieces of stiff plastic

2. Keep in mind that you will modify and change your barge design several times during this unit.

BUILDING BARGES

BUILDING BARGE 1

1. Use the ounce of clay to form a sturdy barge to carry pennies. It should float on top of the water.

2. Use the other materials provided in order to strengthen your barge.

3. Launch your barge in the water. If it sinks, make adjustments until it floats.

4. What did you do to modify your vessel?

_____

_____

5. Observe how your barge floats.

Does it lean?   **YES   NO**   Does it wobble?   **YES   NO**

Is it above water or is it floating low? _____

TEST IT—HOW MANY PENNIES CAN IT HOLD?

1. Place pennies on the barge. Add them slowly. The goal is to see how many pennies the barge can hold before it sinks.

2. Try to arrange pennies on your craft so that it keeps floating. Sketch how you plan to place the pennies in the box on the right.

   THINK: Is it best to place the pennies in the middle or at one of the ends?

   _____

   Which works better on your craft: piling the pennies up or spreading them out?

   _____

3. Slowly add more pennies a few at a time. Count the pennies as you add them. As the barge starts to fill or to wobble, slow down. Add one penny at a time. Keep counting.

4. Remove the pennies and the barge from the water once the barge sinks.

5. How many pennies were you able to load on the barge before it sank? Record this number onto the Barge Trials chart on the following page.

PENNIES

BUILDING BARGES

BARGE 2 DESIGN—TRIAL 2

1. Review the list of materials that can be used. Are there any adjustments you wish to make to your barge to make it stronger and better able to hold pennies?

   _____

   _____

2. Make changes to your barge design and illustrate your revised and rebuilt barge below:

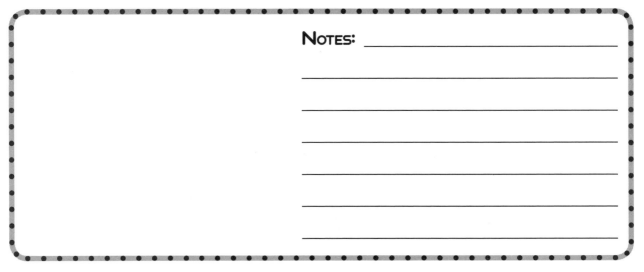

NOTES: _____

_____

_____

_____

_____

_____

_____

3. Retest the modified barge. Add pennies slowly and carefully.

4. On the chart below, record the number of pennies the modified barge held.

5. Discuss your results. Where was the best place to put the pennies?

BARGE TRIALS		
Trial	**Number of Pennies**	**Weight (Each penny weighs 2.5 grams.)**
Barge 1	_____	_____ (____ × 2.5 = _____)
Barge 2	_____	_____ (____ × 2.5 = _____)
Notes and Observations		
_____		
_____		
_____		

BUILDING BARGES

TEAMING UP

1. Team up with another person or team and test your barges together.
2. Share information and ideas, and repair the barges where needed.
3. Combine your materials and work together to create a larger or stronger barge.
4. Sketch the design for the new, team barge below. List the materials used.

· TEAM BARGE DESIGN ·

Materials Used: _____

_____

FINAL BARGE DESIGN TRIAL

1. Build the team barge and test it.
2. On the chart below, record the number of pennies the team barge held.
3. Adjust and improve the team barge.
4. Retest the team barge and record the information for the second trial below.

TEAM BARGE TRIALS		
Trial	**Number of Pennies**	**Weight (Each penny weighs 2.5 grams.)**
1	_____	_____ (____ × 2.5 = _____)
2	_____	_____ (____ × 2.5 = _____)
Notes and Observations		

_____

_____

BUILDING BARGES

JOURNAL ENTRY

1. Which vessel design was the most successful one you made? _____

   _____

   Why did it work well? **THINK:** Did it carry more weight, float better, or was it easier to build?

   _____

   _____

   _____

2. Which extra materials did you add to the clay to help the vessel float? _____

   _____

   How did they help? _____

   _____

3. Which extra materials were the trickiest to use in helping your vessel float? Explain why.

   _____

   _____

4. Why are pennies good materials to use for weights?

   _____

   _____

   What other materials might work? _____

5. What was the most difficult problem you had in making these vessels? _____

   _____

   How did you solve this problem? _____

   _____

   _____

DESIGN PROCESS REVIEW—BUILDING BARGES

Share your journal entries and experiences with your classmates in a class discussion moderated by your teacher.

CREATING FOIL RAFTS

TEACHER PREPARATION: Students may work alone or in pairs to do this activity. Warn students that aluminum foil is very fragile and tears easily. Cut the 4" squares needed ahead of time. Have enough extra squares for those who tear their foil and to allow for about 3 squares per person. Explain that their sketches and trial results will be recorded on the second page of Activity 3.

TEAM MATERIALS

- 4" squares of heavy-duty aluminum foil (3 per student, plus extras)
- 12" rulers
- 20 or more pennies for each student
- water tubs, such as dishpans or bussing trays (Tubs should be at least 3" deep.)

FOIL RAFT–TRIAL 1

Your mission is to build a foil raft and see how many pennies you can float on it.

1. Carefully fold up $\frac{1}{4}$ inch of foil on each side of one of your squares in order to make a vessel to float the pennies. Be careful; it won't work if you tear the foil! Draw your foil raft on page 36 in the first column.

2. Gently place the foil raft in the water. Check that there are no leaks.

3. Carefully place a penny on the foil raft.

4. Slowly and carefully, add more pennies to the vessel, spreading the weight over the surface. Keep track of the number of pennies.

5. Keep adding and counting pennies until the raft collapses and sinks.

6. Record how many pennies your first raft held before sinking. Use the recording sheet on page 36.

FOIL RAFT–TRIAL 2

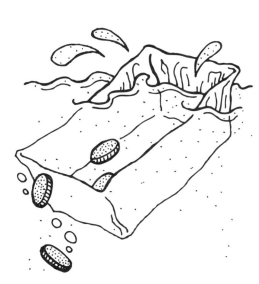

1. Carefully take the vessel from Trial 1 out of the tub and pour out the water. If it is not badly torn, make the bottom of the raft a little smaller by raising the sides to about $\frac{3}{4}$ inch of foil on each side. If your foil raft is totally destroyed, get a second piece of foil and rebuild the raft following the same directions.

2. Draw your revised raft on page 36 in the second column.

3. Slowly and carefully load the foil vessel with pennies again. Keep adding and counting pennies until the vessel sinks.

4. Record how many pennies your second raft held. Add your information to the Foil Raft Trials recording sheet on the bottom of page 36.

CREATING FOIL RAFTS

RAFT DESIGNS

TRIAL 1	TRIAL 2	TRIAL 3

FOIL RAFT—TRIAL 3

1. Carefully take the second foil raft out of the tub and pour out the water. If it is not badly torn, make the sides about 1" high. If your raft is destroyed, get another piece of foil and make a new raft with higher sides. Sketch the raft for Trial 3 above in the third column.

2. Conduct a third trial to see how many pennies the foil raft will hold. Slowly and carefully load your raft again. Keep a careful count of each penny added.

3. Keep adding and counting pennies until the raft collapses and sinks.

4. Record the number of pennies from the third trial below. Compare the three trials.

FOIL RAFT TRIALS

TRIAL	SIDE HEIGHT	NUMBER OF PENNIES	WEIGHT
1	**Low** ($\frac{1}{4}$ inch)		(_____ × 2.5 = _____)
2	**Medium** ($\frac{3}{4}$ inch)		(_____ × 2.5 = _____)
3	**High** (1 inch)		(_____ × 2.5 = _____)

5. Which raft held the most pennies?   **TRIAL   1   2   3**

6. Why do you think that foil raft held so many pennies at one time? _____

_____

CREATING FOIL RAFTS

JOURNAL ENTRY

1. Which material was harder to work with: the clay from Activities 1 and 2 or the foil from Activity 3? Explain your answer.

_____

_____

_____

2. Was there any way to protect the foil from tearing?   **YES   NO**

   Explain. _____

   _____

   _____

3. Which type of vessel was better for holding pennies?   **BOAT   BARGE   RAFT**

   Why? _____

   _____

4. The surface area of a vessel is the outermost layer of the vessel. Explain how changing the part of your vessel that touched the water helped hold more pennies.

   _____

   _____

   _____

5. Which was the most interesting experiment you did today? _____

   Why? _____

   _____

   _____

DESIGN PROCESS REVIEW—CREATING FOIL RAFTS

Share your journal entries, documents, and experiences with aluminum-foil rafts with your classmates in a discussion moderated by your teacher.

NAME _____

CHALLENGE: DESIGN YOUR OWN FLOATING VESSEL

Directions: Use the steps in the Design Process to design the best floating vessel to carry pennies. Refer to the Design Process mini poster (page 4) and the Design Process Worksheet page(s).

BRAINSTORM: Think about the vessels you have made in the Boats and Barges unit. What type of vessel can you build with the materials you have? Remember that your goal is to build a vessel that will carry the most pennies without sinking.

What shape will you make, and why? _____

_____

What materials will you use? _____

_____

Where did your idea come from? Explain. _____

_____

DESIGN THE SOLUTION: Sketch your idea for a vessel in the frame below.

BUILD: Use materials from Activities 1–3 to make your new vessel. Try to construct the best vessel to carry pennies. Use available materials from previous projects and add new ones if approved. Launch your vessel and load it up!

EVALUATE: Does your vessel float? **YES NO**

How many pennies did it carry?

In the space on the right, show how you loaded the pennies onto your vessel. Draw the shape of the base of your vessel and mark where the pennies were placed.

CHALLENGE: DESIGN YOUR OWN FLOATING VESSEL

MODIFY: Make any adjustments or improvements needed to your floating vessel. Sketch the vessel below. Describe the adjustments you made to make the vessel float better and/or to carry more pennies.

NOTES: _____

_____

_____

_____

_____

_____

_____

_____

_____

Does your vessel float now?　　**YES**　　**NO**

How many pennies did your improved vessel carry?

Did your improved vessel carry more pennies?　　**YES**　　**NO**

Why do you think you got that result? _____

_____

Describe how you placed the pennies. _____

_____

SHARE: What other materials would you have liked to use? _____

_____

What would you do differently next time? _____

_____

Discuss with classmates what worked and what did not work.

UNIT 2

WORKING WITH SOUND

5 sessions: 1 session for each activity (approximately 1 to $1\frac{1}{2}$ hours per session)

Focus: Physical Science/Physics—working with sound

CONNECTIONS AND SUGGESTIONS

SCIENCE—This unit explores the structure of the ear and how auditory nerves are stimulated by vibrations that come from moving objects or the air. Students will be learning how these vibrations, or sound waves, create the sounds we hear.

Different ways to create vibrations will be explored using fishing line, cups, paper tubes, rubber bands, and other materials. Students will make aides for hearing, telephones, megaphones, and a variety of instruments to expand their understanding of sound and vibrations.

TECHNOLOGY APPLICATIONS—Students can use computers or personal tablets to do research on sound, hearing, and devices that produce or transmit sound.

Students may digitally record research notes, ideas, and responses as they create a variety of listening devices and musical instruments. They might also take photographs or film their explorations in order to compare the results of their various engineering designs.

ENGINEERING—Students work through the design process to make products that create sounds, magnify sounds, and/or transmit them. They will create and use musical instruments and telephones to explore vibrations caused by different types of objects. Students will need to measure the effects of different actions and materials and make judgments about the utility of each material used.

MATH—Students will be measuring different solid materials in order to create products. They will use addition and subtraction to aid in the creation of listening devices and musical instruments.

DISCUSSION PROMPT: How do we hear sounds? For instance, how does the sound of a siren get from the fire engine to your ears?

Sounds, or sound waves, are invisible waves. We can't see them but we hear the vibrations created when an object moves, or vibrates. When the vibrating object causes the air (or material) around it to move, it creates waves known as sound waves. These waves, or vibrations, travel to our ears and then to our brains. Our brains translate the vibrations into the sounds we know. Our ears have three main parts that work together to help us hear. (See page 43.)

EXTENSION: Have students take turns flapping rulers or dropping unbreakable objects on their desks in order to feel and hear the vibrations. Ask them to lay their heads on their desks to see if it makes a difference in the sounds. Compare the sounds of heavier and lighter items.

WORKING WITH SOUND

UNIT MATERIALS (for a class of 30 to 35)

- ☐ 10 or 12 oz. plastic cups
- ☐ balloons (large, small, and long)
- ☐ cans or bowls
- ☐ colored markers or pencils
- ☐ construction paper
- ☐ fishing line (8-pound test or higher)
- ☐ food coloring
- ☐ glass bottles or jars
- ☐ index cards
- ☐ masking tape
- ☐ metal spoons
- ☐ milk cartons ($\frac{1}{2}$ gallon cardboard, not plastic)
- ☐ newspaper or newsprint
- ☐ paper clips (large and small)
- ☐ paper towel tubes

- ☐ plastic or rubber funnels
- ☐ plastic dinner knives
- ☐ plastic wrap
- ☐ pushpins
- ☐ rice or beans
- ☐ rubber bands (thin and long)
- ☐ rulers
- ☐ scissors
- ☐ tag board
- ☐ towels
- ☐ tuning fork (optional)
- ☐ twine, yarn, or string (optional)
- ☐ water
- ☐ wrapping-paper tubes (optional)

FIND OUT MORE

Phil Tulga—Music Through the Curriculum

Try a virtual water xylophone and learn more about making your own.

http://www.philtulga.com/water.html#5-note

Steve Spangler Science—Bottle Music

https://www.youtube.com/watch?v=at5hnotr1vo

PBS Learning Media

Search "visualize vibrations" to find a number of appropriate videos for this unit.

http://www.pbslearningmedia.org/

The Interactive Ear: *A Guide to Human Hearing*

http://www.amplifon.co.uk/interactive-ear/index.html

Safety Note: All websites should be checked prior to student viewing to be certain that content is appropriate.

WORKING WITH SOUND VOCABULARY

amplify—to make a sound louder

communicate—share or exchange information, news, or ideas

diagonal—a line drawn between opposite corners

eavesdropping—listening in on a private conversation (for example, on a party line)

megaphone—a device for making a voice sound louder

muffle—to make a sound quieter; to decrease sound

notches—marks cut on a piece of material, such as wood or cardboard

orchestra—a large group of musicians who play instruments together, usually guided by a conductor

party line—a telephone line that is shared by multiple households

slack—not stretched or not held in a tight position

sound waves—a series of vibrations that can be heard

taut—tight, with no slack in the line

vibration—a series of rapid back-and-forth or side-to-side movements

Slack and **taut** can be opposites when describing the way a line or a string is being held. Use the correct word to label each picture below.

_____   _____

WORKING WITH SOUND

EARS

Ears are pretty amazing. Ears pick up invisible sound waves, process them, and send the information to the brain. They allow us to hear the world around us. We hear loud sounds like sirens, and we hear quieter sounds, like birds chirping. We can hear people talking and we can listen to music. We can tell the difference between the sound of an ice cream truck and a dog barking. But how do ears work?

Ears have three main parts. These three parts work together to help us hear:

1. You can see and touch most of the **outer ear**. This part leads to the ear canal and ends at the eardrum. Vibrations enter the ear through the outer ear.

2. The **middle ear** starts at the eardrum. The eardrum vibrates. It has the three little bones that carry the sound vibrations to the inner ear.

3. The **inner ear** changes the vibrations into signals for the brain. These signals are the sounds we hear.

Our ears do very important work for us and need to be protected. You can protect your ears from very loud sounds by turning down the volume or by wearing earplugs.

Label the three parts of the ear in the diagram below.

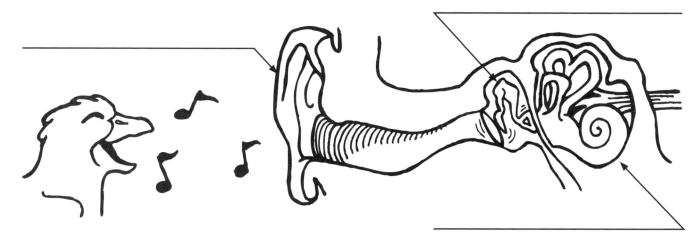

EARS HELP US KEEP OUR BALANCE

Have you ever gotten dizzy? If you have, it is because of your inner ear. If you move too fast or spin around too long and then stop quickly, you might feel wobbly. You feel dizzy or off balance. This is because there are fluids in your inner ear that keep moving even though you have stopped.

You might also feel dizzy if you have an ear infection.

WORKING WITH SOUND

VIBRATIONS

A vibration is a movement. A vibration can move side to side or up and down. Vibrations make the sounds we hear and come from many sources. Look closely at the string of a guitar when it is plucked. You can hear the sound as you watch it vibrate.

All musical instruments use vibrations to create sounds. Other vibrations are made when you clap your hands. If you hold your throat when you hum, you will feel vibrations.

How do our ears help us hear things? The bones, hairs, and nerves in our ears work together to pick up invisible sound waves or pressure waves. The vibrations make the sounds we hear.

The stronger a vibration is, the louder the sound will be. The engine of an airplane will make a louder sound than the engine of a car. This is because the airplane engine is larger and moves more air as it vibrates, creating stronger vibrations.

TEST IT—SEE THE VIBRATIONS!

1. Find a drum or make one by stretching a big balloon over a bowl or can.

2. Put rice or other small objects on the top of the drum and tap it.

3. What happens to the small objects?

_____

_____

Do they bounce?   **YES   NO**

> That is a vibration! The *vibration* is what causes the sound the drum makes.

4. Can you find other things that vibrate?

_____   _____   _____

AMPLIFYING SOUNDS

Directions: Work in teams of two to demonstrate the fact that when sound is concentrated and focused toward the human ear, it is easier to hear. Some sounds seem louder because other sounds are blocked.

TEAM MATERIALS
- 18" × 12" construction paper or tag board (one per student)
- masking tape
- markers or colored pencils
- paper towel tubes (one per student)
- plastic wrap
- rubber bands
- scissors

MAKE A HEARING AID

1. Find a clean, dry paper towel tube and hold the tube against your ear.

2. Ask your partner to whisper something into the tube and then to speak in a normal voice into the tube.

3. Compare your partner's whisper to his or her normal voice. Describe the difference.

_____

_____

4. How well did you hear your partner's voice?

CLEARLY   **WITH DIFFICULTY**   **COULDN'T HEAR**

MODIFY AND TEST THE HEARING AID

1. Fold a piece of plastic wrap around one end of the tube. Make the wrap tight over the opening. Hold the plastic wrap in place by holding the edges down with a tight rubber band.

2. While you hold the tube next to your ear, have your partner tap lightly on the plastic wrap with his or her fingernail or a pencil. Describe the sound you hear.

   THINK: Is the sound clear?   **YES**   **NO**   Is the sound loud?   **YES**   **NO**

   How would you describe it? _____

_____

3. Why do you think the tube (covered or uncovered) helps you hear some sounds better?

_____

_____

AMPLIFYING SOUNDS

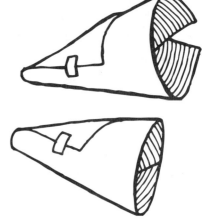

MAKE A MEGAPHONE

1. You can make a communication device with a piece of paper! Fold a piece of 18" × 12" construction paper or tag board into a spiral to make a megaphone as shown on the right.

2. Tape the spiral in place to stabilize the megaphone shape. The small end should be somewhere between the size of a penny and the size of the paper towel tube opening.

3. Bend or cut the extra paper so the large end of the spiral is a wide, circular opening with even edges.

4. Write short messages to send to your partner.

MESSAGE 1 _____

_____

MESSAGE 2 _____

_____

TEST THE MEGAPHONE

...16, 17, 18...

1. Take your megaphone outdoors or into a large, open room such as an assembly hall or gym. Have your partner count off 20 paces and turn to face you.

2. Send your message to your partner using the megaphone. Use a regular voice. Do not yell.

3. Listen to your partner's message. Write down what you heard.

MESSAGE 1 _____

_____

4. Move another 20 paces away from your partner, or each team member can move back 10 paces. Send and receive your second message. Write down what you heard.

MESSAGE 2 _____

_____

5. Check with the person who sent you each message. Did you understand each message clearly?

MESSAGE 1   YES   NO   MESSAGE 2   YES   NO

Why? _____

_____

 NAME _____

AMPLIFYING SOUNDS

JOURNAL ENTRY

1. Explain how the paper towel hearing aid helped you hear sounds.

_____

_____

_____

_____

2. How are the hearing aid and the megaphone alike?

_____

_____

_____

_____

3. Which worked better for you?   **HEARING AID   MEGAPHONE**
   Why?

_____

_____

4. Now that you know that sounds are created by vibrations, name two sounds you can make by creating vibrations.

   SOUND 1 _____

   SOUND 2 _____

5. Name two sounds you like to hear. _____   _____

6. Name two sounds you don't like to hear. _____   _____

DESIGN PROCESS REVIEW—AMPLIFYING SOUNDS

Share your journal entries, documents, and experiences making hearing aids and megaphones with your classmates in a discussion moderated by your teacher.

MAKING TELEPHONES

Directions: Work in pairs in order to create plastic cup telephones.

> **TEAM MATERIALS**
> - 10- or 12-ounce plastic drinking cups or yogurt cups (one per student)
> - fishing line (8-pound strength or higher)
> - masking tape
> - paper clips
> - pushpins

MAKING PLASTIC CUP TELEPHONES

1. You can make a very effective communication device by using fishing line and 2 plastic cups. Use a pushpin to make a small hole in the center of the bottom of each plastic cup.
2. Cut a piece of fishing line the length of the room or longer, preferably 50 or 60 feet.
3. Feed one end of the fishing line through the hole that is in the bottom of the cup.
4. Tie the fishing line to a paper clip (large or small). Tie the knot several times so the line doesn't slip off.
5. Do the same thing to the bottom of the other cup by using the other end of the fishing line.

NOTE: If the telephones are assembled correctly and the fishing line is kept *taut*, you should be able to communicate clearly back and forth in a "long distance" conversation. The speaker's voice should create vibrations in the bottom of the cup that you should be able to hear with your ear close to the cup's opening.

TESTING PLASTIC CUP TELEPHONES

1. You and your partner need to find an outdoor space that allows enough space to stretch the plastic cup phone until the fishing line is taut (tight).

2. One of you needs to be the listener and to hold the cup over your ear.
3. The speaker needs to speak directly into the cup in order to make the bottom vibrate. Remember to keep the line taut at all times.
4. The speaker can start out by asking if the listener can hear him or her clearly. Record the response. **YES   NO**
5. Get familiar with the phone by carrying on a conversation for a few minutes about school, science, sports, or similar subjects.

★ ★ ★ **SAVE THE TELEPHONES FOR A FUTURE ACTIVITY** ★ ★ ★

(N)(A)(M)(E) _____

MAKING TELEPHONES

JOURNAL ENTRY

1. While you are speaking to your partner, pinch the fishing line with your thumb and forefinger. Describe what happens.

   _____

   _____

2. While you are listening to your partner, keep the fishing line taut. Hold your forefinger against the fishing line. What do you feel as you touch the line?

   _____

   _____

3. Could you still hear your partner when you held your forefinger and thumb against the fishing line? How did the message sound?

   ☐ CLEAR AND UNDERSTANDABLE

   ☐ MUFFLED SOUND, BUT UNDERSTANDABLE

   ☐ HEARD SOUND, BUT COULDN'T UNDERSTAND

   ☐ COULD NOT HEAR ANYTHING

4. Move so that your "phone line" is touching a tree or pole or another obstacle while you are talking with your partner.

   Describe the obstacle.

   _____

   _____

   Could either of you hear when the "phone line" was touching the obstacle?   **YES   NO**

   Explain: _____

   _____

5. List the conditions under which you couldn't hear each other:

   a. _____

   b. _____

   c. _____

   d. _____

NAME _____

MAKING TELEPHONES

Directions: Combine with another team. You will need four people in order to create a party line telephone system.

PARTY-LINE CONVERSATIONS

The telephone was invented by Alexander Graham Bell in 1876. Within 10 years, there were more than 150,000 phones in operation. Until the 1980s, many people in rural communities still had party lines. Someone in every house on the party line would answer the phone until they knew who the call was for. Every neighbor could listen in on conversations. All the telephone operators who worked for the phone company listened too.

Most party lines were discontinued in the 1980s because the Internet and other devices couldn't be used on a party line.

MAKE YOUR OWN PARTY LINE

1. Make your own "party line" by teaming up with another group so that you have a team of four people.

2. Stand so that you are facing your partner at a distance. One member of the other team is on your right—halfway between you and your partner. The other member of the other team is on your left—halfway between you and your partner.

3. Loop the fishing line once from one team's phone over the other team's line. Make sure all four members of the party line keep their lines taut.

4. Three team members should be listening with their plastic cups to their ears. One member should be talking into his or her plastic-cup telephone.

5. Let each partner take a turn talking and answering questions. Remember to keep the telephone lines taut and to talk into the cup.

6. Could you hear clearly? **YES   NO   SOMETIMES**

LARGER PARTY LINES

1. Encourage another team to join your conversation by looping their line over the two lines already there. Keep the lines taut.

2. Can five people hear when the sixth person is talking? **YES   NO**

   How well could you hear? _____

   _____

MAKING TELEPHONES

JOURNAL ENTRY

1. Which activity was more successful?   **CUP PHONES**   **PARTY LINES**

   Why? _____

   _____

2. Could you feel the vibrations in the cup or the line?   **YES**   **NO**

   Explain: _____

   _____

3. **Hypothesize:** What is the longest length of fishing line that could be used that would still allow messages to be heard clearly through the plastic cups?

   _____

   _____

4. What materials might work even better than the 8-ounce or 10-ounce plastic cups you used?

   _____

   Explain your answer. _____

   _____

5. How would you feel if you had to use a party line? Explain. _____

   _____

   _____

6. What experiment with sound would you like to try? _____

   _____

   _____

   _____

DESIGN PROCESS REVIEW—MAKING TELEPHONES

Share your experiences, observations, journals, and other documents about working with sound with your classmates in a class discussion led and moderated by your teacher.

NAME _____

CREATING A GUITAR

Directions: Work in pairs in order to make guitars. Use standard and metric rulers.

> ### TEAM MATERIALS
> - clean, half-gallon, cardboard milk cartons
> - 4 large, long rubber bands per carton
> - masking tape
> - pencils, markers
> - plastic knives
> - rulers—centimeter and inch
> - tag board or 4" × 6" index cards
> - scissor or knife (with adult assistance)

MAKING THE MILK CARTON GUITAR

1. Tape the hole closed or staple the opening of the milk carton shut.

2. Measure the very top of the milk carton with a ruler. Use a pen to make a mark every 2 centimeters across the top seam of the carton.

3. Use a plastic knife to carve small grooves at the 2 cm, 4 cm, 6 cm, and 8 cm marks. If this does not work, ask an adult to use a scissor or knife to help make the grooves.

4. Mark the 4" × 6" inch index card the long way at every inch.

5. Carefully fold the end to the 1" mark and crease the fold. Then continue folding at each inch mark. You will have six even, sharply-creased folds—each 1" long.

MAKING THE BRIDGE

1. Fold the first inch to the third inch in order to make a triangular-prism shape. Then fold the 4th section over the 1st, the 5th over the 2nd, and the 6th over the 3rd section. You now have a triangular prism that is two cards thick. Place a piece of tape along the end of the card to hold the prism in place.

2. Make marks along the edge of the prism at 2 cm, 4 cm, 6 cm, and 8 cm.

3. Use a plastic knife in order to carve a small groove into the prism at each mark. Ask for adult help if needed.

4. Place this guitar bridge near the top of the carton, about 1" below where the carton is angled. Make sure that the bridge is straight.

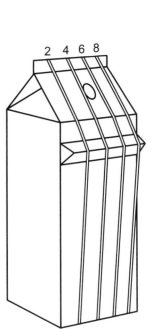

ADDING GUITAR STRINGS

1. Position four rubber bands around the milk carton the long way.

2. Place the four bands in the grooves that are on the top of the carton and on the bridge.

3. Reposition the bridge if necessary.

CREATING A GUITAR

PLAYING YOUR INSTRUMENT

1. Strum your milk carton guitar several times.

   Can you feel the vibrations? **YES   NO**

2. Use your forefinger to flick or to pluck each string.

3. Try picking two rubber bands at the same time. Try different combinations: the first and fourth, the second and third, and so forth.

4. Spend some time developing your own sound.

CHANGING THE TONE

1. Try to change the sound or pitch of your instrument. Adjust the bridge or the rubber bands.

   Explain what you did. _____

   _____

   _____

2. Cut away an oval-shaped opening about one inch from the bridge, two inches long toward the bottom of the instrument. Take a look at a real guitar to get a better idea of the opening's placement.

3. What do you notice about the sound of the guitar now?

   _____

   _____

CREATING A GUITAR

JOURNAL ENTRY

1. What was the most difficult part about making the guitar? _____

_____

_____

2. How might you improve the guitar? _____

_____

_____

3. Could you fit 5 rubber bands (strings) on the milk carton?   **YES**   **NO**

   What would you have to do? _____

_____

_____

4. Do you think thinner rubber bands would have provided a different sound?   **YES   NO**

   Why or why not? _____

_____

5. Were you able to create different sounds with each rubber band as you played the guitar?

   YES   NO

   Explain your answer. _____

_____

6. What did you learn about vibrations by doing this activity? _____

_____

_____

_____

DESIGN PROCESS REVIEW—CREATING A GUITAR

Share your experiences, observations, documents, and journal entries about building guitars with your classmates in a discussion led by your teacher.

MUSIC WITH BOTTLES

TEAM MATERIALS

- 8 clear glass bottles or drinking glasses (sizes can vary)
- food coloring
- funnels
- markers or colored pencils
- metal spoons
- ruler
- towels, newspaper, or absorbent mats
- water

TEACHER PREPARATION: Arrange areas where students can work with water. Discuss safety issues when working with the glass bottles.

SETTING UP THE BOTTLES

1. Carefully arrange the eight glass bottles in a line on a towel, newspaper, or a mat. If the bottles are different sizes, arrange them by size with the tallest bottle at one end and the shortest on the other end.

2. Start at the end that has the shortest bottle and use a funnel to add 1" water to the first bottle and 2" of water to the second bottle. (Either end will work if the bottles are the same size.)

3. Add one more inch of water to each bottle. The last bottle should have 8 inches of water.

4. Use food coloring to color the water in each bottle. Mix your own colors or make a rainbow using the "recipe" below.

Bottle 1—4 drops of red food coloring

Bottle 2—1 drop of red food coloring and 2 drops of yellow to make orange

Bottle 3—4 drops of yellow food coloring

Bottle 4—2 drops of blue food coloring and 2 drops of yellow to make green

Bottle 5—2 drops of blue food coloring

Bottle 6—3 drops of blue and 1 drop of red to make indigo (dark blue)

Bottle 7—2 drops of blue and 2 drops of red to make violet (lighter than purple)

Bottle 8—leave water clear or create a color and fit it into the rainbow.

5. Sketch the final row of containers showing the heights of the water and the colors used.

MUSIC WITH BOTTLES

PLAYING THE BOTTLES

1. Use a metal spoon to tap each bottle in the middle. Do you hear different sounds?

   YES   NO

   Describe the different sounds you hear.

   _____

   _____

2. Now tap each bottle near the bottom and then near the top.   Does it make a difference in the sounds you hear when you hit the bottles at different heights? Explain.

   _____

   _____

3. Move from one end of the row of bottles to the other and back. Listen to the sounds created by the vibrations. What do you notice?

   _____

   _____

4. If you tap each bottle, starting with the one with the least amount of water and ending with the one with the most water, what do you notice happening to the sound?

   _____

   _____

5. Now do the reverse. Start with the bottle that is holding the most water and end with the bottle having least amount of water. What do you notice? Is the sound the same or different?

   _____

   Explain. _____

   _____

VARIATIONS

1. Adjust the water levels or rearrange the bottles to create different sounds.
2. Make a personal set of bottles so that you can blow over the tops to create different sounds (without spreading germs!).

MUSIC WITH BOTTLES

JOURNAL ENTRY

1. What was the most surprising thing about playing the bottles?

_____

_____

_____

_____

2. Did the types of sounds change if you played the bottles at the top, in the middle, or at the bottom?

_____

_____

_____

_____

3. What causes the vibrations when you play bottles? _____

_____

Explain. _____

_____

_____

_____

4. What adjustments did you make to the water levels to create different sounds?

_____

_____

_____

_____

DESIGN PROCESS REVIEW—MUSIC WITH BOTTLES

Share your observations, experiences, documentation, and journal entries about bottle music with your classmates in a discussion led by your teacher.

CHALLENGE: DESIGN YOUR OWN SOUND DEVICE

Directions: Use the steps in the Design Process to make a device to demonstrate how vibrations create sound.

BRAINSTORM: Think about the products you have made that convey sound. Would you like to make a better communications device or a type of musical instrument? Remember, your goal is to convey sound through vibrations.

What type of product will you make? _____

_____

What materials will you use? _____

_____

Where is your inspiration coming from? _____

_____

Will you need to do more research?   **YES   NO**

If so, what will you look up? _____

DESIGN THE SOLUTION: Sketch your ideas below. Add notes.

NOTES: _____

_____

_____

_____

_____

_____

_____

_____

BUILD: Construct your sound device using materials from Activities 1–4. List any problems that arise.

_____

_____

_____

CHALLENGE: DESIGN YOUR OWN SOUND DEVICE

EVALUATE: Does your sound device work the way you planned?   **YES   NO**

What needs adjusting or improving? _____

_____

_____

Can you feel the vibrations? _____

_____

_____

How does your device work? _____

_____

_____

MODIFY: Describe the adjustments you made to improve your sound device.

_____

_____

_____

SHARE: What do you call your device? _____

_____

_____

What does your device do? _____

_____

_____

Discuss what worked and what needs to be improved upon. _____

_____

_____

_____

What surprised you the most about sound? _____

_____

_____

 **3**

SOLUTIONS, MIXTURES, AND EMULSIONS

5 sessions: one session for each activity (approximately 1 to $1\frac{1}{2}$ hours per session)

Focus: Physical Science—chemistry

CONNECTIONS AND SUGGESTIONS

SCIENCE—Students will be chemists and will implement the scientific method. They will be making solutions, mixtures, and emulsions by using liquids. Some of these combinations will be *solutions*, meaning that all the ingredients will mix or blend together and others will be *mixtures*, where some of the added ingredients do not blend together. They will also be creating *emulsions*, which are ingredients that ordinarily form mixtures but can be blended—at least for a short time—by adding *emulsifiers*. Students will add to their science vocabulary and knowledge by answering the following questions through a variety of explorations:

1. What is the difference between a *solution* and a *mixture*?

2. What does an *emulsifier* like soap or mustard do to a mixture?

TECHNOLOGY—Students may use computers, tablets, cameras and/or video equipment to record their observations of actions and reactions as they mix and blend ingredients. They may wish to use technology to describe the problems encountered, the solutions attempted, and the success rate of each activity.

ENGINEERING—Students will be using specific materials and tools to make a variety of solutions, mixtures, and emulsions. They should be encouraged to use the design process and experiment with ways to improve the measuring and pouring processes.

Encourage students to determine the best way to shake the bottles used and to figure out ways to stabilize the bottles between activities. They will share their findings during the unit's *Scientific Method Review* and use them in their final unit challenge.

MATH—Students will be working with units of liquid measure (ounces) and solid measures (teaspoons) to make solutions, mixtures, and emulsions. The measurement applications in this unit require that students be systematic and specific about the precise amounts of materials used in creating solutions, mixtures, and emulsions.

> **DISCUSSION PROMPT:** What does a chemist do?
>
> Chemists study solids, liquids, and gases. A chemist solves problems using math, science, and technology. A chemist sees a problem and tries to fix it. A chemist might try to find a medicine to help cure an illness or might come up with a way to make food stay fresh longer. One way chemists do this is by working with solutions, mixtures, and emulsions.

SOLUTIONS, MIXTURES, AND EMULSIONS

UNIT MATERIALS (for a class of 30 to 35)

- ☐ 33 oz. or larger clear plastic bottles with caps
- ☐ 6" paper circles
- ☐ 12 oz. and 16 oz. plastic bottles with caps
- ☐ access to cold, warm, and hot water
- ☐ baby oil
- ☐ baking soda
- ☐ black pepper
- ☐ clear plastic cups
- ☐ colored pencils
- ☐ cooking oil (different types)
- ☐ corn syrup
- ☐ dish soap (Dawn® or Joy®)
- ☐ eyedroppers
- ☐ flour
- ☐ food coloring—red, yellow, blue, and green
- ☐ funnels
- ☐ laundry soap

- ☐ magnifying glasses
- ☐ measuring cups
- ☐ paper towels
- ☐ permanent markers
- ☐ plastic spoons
- ☐ rock salt and table salt
- ☐ rubbing alcohol
- ☐ rulers
- ☐ scissors
- ☐ stopwatches or timers
- ☐ sugar
- ☐ tape
- ☐ trays or tubs
- ☐ vinegar
- ☐ water
- ☐ white paper

FIND OUT MORE

Louis Pasteur *http://www.biography.com/people/louis-pasteur-9434402*

Mixture Basics *http://www.chem4kids.com/files/matter_mixture.html*

How to Build a Road Using Roller Compacted Concrete (CEMEXUSA)

http://www.youtube.com/watch?v=mcDxw2HLLS8

This video shows "ingredients" of concrete and the machinery used to mix concrete and form roads. It demonstrates STEM at work.

Safety Note: All websites should be checked prior to student viewing to be certain that content is appropriate.

Solutions, Mixtures, and Emulsions Vocabulary

chemist—a person who studies solids, liquids, and gases to solve problems

chemistry—the branch of science that identifies the substances that compose matter; the study of the way materials interact, combine, and change

density—how much matter is in a certain volume—all matter has density

diffuse—to spread out within a solution or an area; to scatter

dissolve—to break up, as in a solid breaking into a liquid; when something dissolves, it seems to disappear
Example: stirring sugar into coffee

emulsify—to blend, shake, or mix together to make an emulsion

emulsifier—a material which is used to combine or blend two other materials in an emulsion

emulsion—a solution formed with substances that do not usually mix

ingredient—any food or substance that is combined to make something new or different

mixture—a combination of two or more substances that do not blend to create a new substance (example: sand and water)

reaction—a response; a chemical change

solution—a special type of mixture in which two or more items mixed together blend to form one substance (example: sugar and water)

Solutions, Mixtures, and Emulsions—What is the difference?

1. **Mixture:** Sand and water do not blend—they remain sand and water when mixed.

2. **Solution:** Lemon juice, sugar, and water blend to make lemonade.

3. **Emulsion:** A salad dressing made of oil and vinegar will not stay blended, but adding mustard will blend the oil and vinegar for a while.

SOLUTIONS, MIXTURES, AND EMULSIONS

WHO KNEW?

LOUIS PASTEUR

LOUIS PASTEUR

Let's look at the work of one chemist, Louis Pasteur. He was a chemist a long time ago. He lived in France in the 1800s. Dr. Pasteur knew how important it was to wash our hands. He knew that if people washed their hands they would not spread as many germs. This means that people would not get as sick. Today, we know how important it is to wash our hands. We try to wash our hands often at home and at school.

He taught doctors to wash their hands. He told doctors to wash their tools in very hot water, too. This made hospitals much safer.

He is also famous for his work with foods. You may have heard the word *pasteurization*. It is named after Dr. Pasteur. It is a process of boiling liquids, like milk, and then cooling them. This process gets rid of germs. This process keeps milk and other foods from spoiling. His work improved people's lives all over the world.

In addition, Dr. Pasteur also studied the germs that made people sick. He made medicines to help people fight these germs. Chemists like Dr. Pasteur help us live healthy lives.

Chemists today continue to try to make life better. The work they do helps keep our foods safe. Some chemists design new medicines. Others work to make our air and water cleaner.

How has chemistry affected your life? _____

_____

_____

_____

_____

SOLUTIONS, MIXTURES, AND EMULSIONS

LET'S BRAINSTORM!

Many occupations need chemists. Chemists study liquids, solids, and gasses to make new products and improve old ones.

Think of jobs that require ingredients to be mixed. How do you think the jobs below use chemistry?

1. **Chefs:** _____
   _____
   _____
   _____
   _____

2. **Perfume makers:** _____
   _____
   _____
   _____
   _____

3. **Pyrotechnics operator** (fireworks displays): _____
   _____
   _____
   _____
   _____

4. **Road builders and pavers:** _____
   _____
   _____
   _____
   _____

WORKING WITH SOLUTIONS AND MIXTURES

TEACHER PREPARATION: Have students work in pairs or small teams. Explain that they will be combining liquids and solids and determining if the combinations are *solutions* or *mixtures*. Working in teams will help with timing and observing different interactions.

Students will also be observing *density*—which is seen in the relationship of the heaviness of the different liquids they use. Remember, heaviness and density are not the same thing.

Review and discuss the vocabulary list together to gain a better understanding of the unit topic. Discuss the meaning of *solution* and *mixture* throughout this unit:

SOLUTION—a special type of mixture in which two or more items mixed together blend to form one item. For instance, when you mix lemon juice, sugar, and water, you get something new—lemonade!

MIXTURE—a combination of two or more substances that do not chemically combine, such as sand and water. You can mix them together, but the sand will not blend into the water; the sand and water will still be two separate substances.

TEAM MATERIALS

- 6" paper circles (for funnels)
- baking soda
- black pepper
- 12 oz. clear plastic bottles with caps
- colored pencils
- cooking oil
- eyedroppers
- food coloring (yellow, blue, red)
- funnels
- measuring cups
- permanent markers
- plastic teaspoons
- scissors
- sugar
- table salt
- tape
- timers or stopwatches
- water

NOTES

Eyedroppers: If using large bottles of food coloring, you will need to provide students with eyedroppers to add coloring to the mixtures. Smaller squeeze bottles of food coloring are made to squeeze a drop at a time.

Measuring Cups: If measuring cups are unavailable, mark 6" clear plastic cups. Use a permanent marker to draw 5 short, evenly-spaced lines on the plastic cups. These will provide a fairly accurate estimate of 5 ounces. (See picture at right.)

Plastic Bottles: The flatter the sides (fewer ripples) of the bottles or jars, the better. The students will be observing reactions in the bottles. Lidded jars may be used as well.

Funnels: Allow each student time to create a funnel (see p.66) before beginning the activities in this unit. Encourage students to consider different types of funnels and funnel designs.

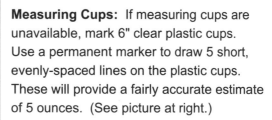

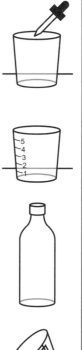

⚠ CAUTIONS

☐ ALWAYS keep hands away from face and eyes when handling chemical compounds.

☐ ALWAYS wash your hands when done.

☐ NEVER drink or taste liquids used in science class.

WORKING WITH SOLUTIONS AND MIXTURES

MAKE A FUNNEL

1. Measure the diameter of the paper circle.
   DIAMETER = _____

2. Mark the middle of the circle. You can fold the paper in quarters to find this. The middle point is half the diameter, which is _____ inches.

3. Cut out a wedge, using the middle of the circle as the point.

4. Wrap the paper to form a cone, and tape it.

5. Snip a small opening that will fit inside the opening of the bottle. This opening may need to be adjusted during the activities.

6. Test the funnel.

7. If time allows, try making more funnels with other types of paper, or use thin plastic sheets which work better for funnels.

GETTING STARTED—MIXING TWO LIQUIDS

1. Measure out 5 ounces of water. Use a funnel to pour the water into an empty plastic water bottle. The bottle should hold at least 12 oz.

2. Squeeze a single drop of food coloring into the water in the bottle. (*Note:* If you have a large bottle of food coloring, use an eyedropper to add the color drop.) Do *not* shake the bottle. Replace the cap.

3. Watch the food coloring **diffuse** (spread) through the water.

4. Describe how the food coloring moved. Use your best descriptive words.

   _____

   _____

5. What do water and food coloring form?

   ### MIXTURE   SOLUTION

6. Use colored pencils to sketch the food coloring diffusing through the water in the bottle to the right.

WORKING WITH SOLUTIONS AND MIXTURES

Directions: Read all the directions before beginning so you will know when you need to stop and start the timers.

ADDING SALT

1. Start the timer when you add a teaspoon of salt to the water and food coloring. Use a funnel to get the salt into the bottle. Watch the salt for 15 seconds. What does it do?

_____

2. Put the cap back on. Lift up the bottle and look up at the bottom. What do you see?

_____

3. About how much salt dissolved on the way down?   **SOME   ALL**
4. Shake the bottle for 15 seconds and then let the contents settle for 60 seconds.
5. About how much of the teaspoon of salt seems to have dissolved?   **SOME   ALL**
6. Sketch the contents of the bottle that is in the bottle below, on the left. Circle whether the ingredients formed a *solution* or a *mixture*.

ADDING SUGAR

1. Add a teaspoon of sugar to the mixture. Observe the sugar. What does it do?

_____

2. Put the cap back on. Lift up the bottle and look up at the bottom. What do you see?

_____

3. About how much sugar dissolved on the way down?   **SOME   ALL**
4. Shake the bottle for 15 seconds and then let the ingredients settle for 60 seconds.
5. About how much of the teaspoon of sugar seems to have dissolved?   **SOME   ALL**
6. Sketch the contents of the bottle in the bottle below that is on the right. Circle whether the ingredients formed a *solution* or a *mixture*.

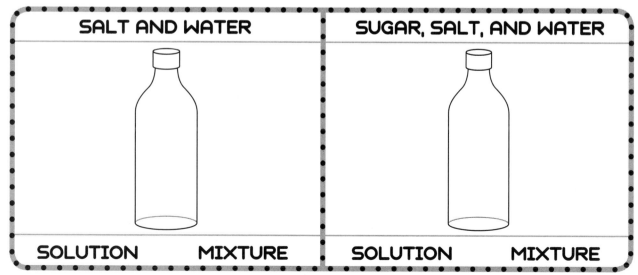

WORKING WITH SOLUTIONS AND MIXTURES

ADDING BAKING SODA

1. Add a teaspoon of baking soda to the bottle that has the salt and sugar. Observe the baking soda falling to the bottom of the bottle. Do you think it will all dissolve? **YES NO**

2. Put the cap back on the bottle and lift it up to look at the bottom. What do you see?

   _____

3. About how much baking soda dissolved on the way down? **SOME ALL**

4. Shake the bottle for 30 seconds and then let the ingredients settle for 60 seconds.

5. About how much of the baking soda dissolved? **SOME ALL**

6. Sketch the bottle and its contents in the bottle below that on the left. Circle whether the ingredients formed a *solution* or a *mixture*.

ADDING BLACK PEPPER

1. Add a teaspoon of black pepper to the bottle. What does the black pepper do?

   _____

2. Put the cap back on the bottle and lift it up to look at the bottom. What do you see?

   _____

3. About how much black pepper dissolved on the way down? **SOME ALL NONE**

4. Shake the bottle for 30 seconds and then let the ingredients settle for 60 seconds.

5. About how much of the teaspoon of black pepper seems to have dissolved?

   SOME ALL NONE

6. Take turns shaking the bottle for 15 seconds each. Any change? **YES NO**

7. Sketch the contents of the bottle in the bottle below that is on the right. Circle whether the ingredients formed a *solution* or a *mixture*.

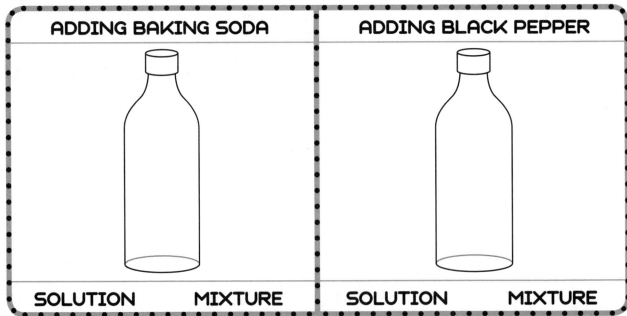

ADDING BAKING SODA	ADDING BLACK PEPPER
SOLUTION MIXTURE	SOLUTION MIXTURE

WORKING WITH SOLUTIONS AND MIXTURES

JOURNAL ENTRY

1. What is a **solution** in chemistry? _____

_____

_____

Give two examples. _____

_____

2. What is a **mixture** in chemistry? _____

_____

_____

Give an example or two. _____

3. When the food coloring was **diffused** in the water, what did it do? _____

_____

_____

4. Do you think funnels are useful when adding ingredients to a mixture?   **YES   NO**

Explain your answer. _____

_____

_____

5. If you were a **chemist**, what type of projects would you like to work on? Why?

_____

_____

_____

_____

SCIENTIFIC METHOD REVIEW—WORKING WITH SOLUTIONS AND MIXTURES

Share your journal entries, documents, and experiences making funnels and working with solutions and mixtures with your class in a discussion moderated by your teacher.

MORE MIXTURES

Directions: Work in pairs. Read through the directions before beginning so you will know when you need to stop and start the timers.

> ### TEAM MATERIALS
> - clear plastic bottles (at least 30 oz.) with caps
> - colored pencils
> - cooking oil
> - eyedroppers
> - food coloring (red, yellow, blue)
> - funnels
> - measuring cups
> - permanent markers
> - plastic teaspoons
> - stopwatch or timer
> - water

GETTING STARTED—MIXING OIL AND WATER

1. Fill a plastic bottle halfway with water.

2. Measure out 2 ounces of cooking oil and use a funnel to add it to the water in the bottle. **Do not shake the bottle!**

3. What does the oil do? _____

   _____

   When combined, what do the two liquids make?

   ### A SOLUTION   A MIXTURE

4. Where does the oil settle? _____

5. Which liquid do you think is denser? _____

   Why? _____

6. In the bottle on the right, sketch what the oil does.

OIL AND WATER

ADDING A DROP OF COLOR

1. Carefully add one or two drops of yellow or red food coloring to the ingredients and start the timer. **Do not shake or disturb the bottle!**

2. What does the food coloring do at first? _____

   _____

3. Observe the color drops. You may have to wait 2–3 minutes to see a change. (Try doing some arm stretches while you wait, but don't take your eyes off the drops!) Stop the timer as soon as the reaction begins.

4. How long did it take? _____

5. Describe and sketch what happened to the food coloring.

   _____

   _____

DROPS BEFORE REACTION

MORE MIXTURES

SHAKE IT UP!

1. Make sure the cap on the bottle is secure. Set the timer again and shake the ingredients for 30 seconds.

2. Use colored pencils to sketch the contents of the bottle.

3. Describe what happens to the oil, water, and food coloring after shaking. _____

_____

4. What type of mixture did you make?

A SOLUTION   A MIXTURE

How do you know? _____

_____

_____

AFTER SHAKING

ADDING A SECOND COLOR

1. Use the oil, water, and color mixture from the previous activity. Make sure it has settled.

2. Carefully add 2 drops of blue food coloring to the ingredients.

3. Set the timer to see how long it takes the color drops to travel through the oil. (Do some side-to-side neck stretches or neck rolls while you watch, but keep your eyes on the drops!)

4. Describe what happens. _____

_____

5. Make sure the cover is on tightly. Set the timer again, and shake the bottle for 15 seconds.

6. Describe what happens to the oil, water, and colors after shaking. _____

_____

7. What color is the mixture now? _____

Use colored pencils to sketch the settled mixture with the second color. Use the bottle in the lower box on the right.

ADDING A
SECOND COLOR

★ ★ ★ SAVE THIS MIXTURE ★ ★ ★

MORE MIXTURES

ADDING WARM WATER

1. Wait for the colored liquid to settle. While you wait, *carefully* measure out 3 ounces of warm water.

2. Use a funnel to add the warm water to the bottle, and put the cap on the bottle again. Describe the reaction.

   _____

   _____

3. Use colored pencils to sketch the results in the box below on the left.

ADDING A THIRD COLOR

1. Set the timer and add a drop of a third color food coloring. (Do some side stretches while you watch, but keep your eyes on the drop!) Stop the timer when a reaction occurs.

2. How long before the reaction of the color and the warm water began? _____

3. Describe the reaction of the color to the warm water. _____

   _____

4. Use colored pencils to sketch the results in the middle box below.

5. Shake the bottle one more time. Let it settle. Describe the results this time. _____

   _____

6. What did you make when you added warm water?   **SOLUTION   MIXTURE**

   How do you know? _____

   _____

7. Use colored pencils to sketch the settled mixture with the third color in the box on the right.

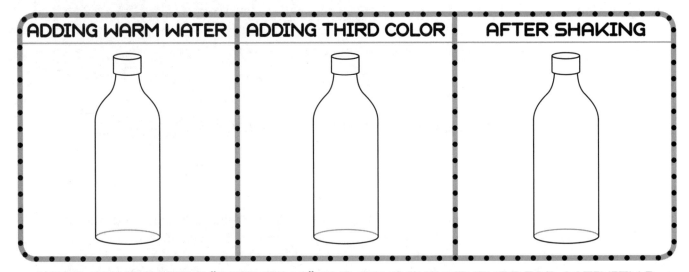

ADDING WARM WATER   ADDING THIRD COLOR   AFTER SHAKING

★ LABEL YOUR BOTTLE "ACTIVITY 2" AND SAVE THE MIXTURE FOR ACTIVITY 3. ★

MORE MIXTURES

JOURNAL ENTRY

1. What was the most unexpected reaction that occurred in your mixture? _____

_____

_____

2. Do oil and water naturally mix?   **YES   NO**

   Explain your answer. _____

   _____

   _____

3. Which material is denser?   **OIL   WATER**

   How do you know? _____

   _____

4. Did the food coloring mix with the oil?   **YES   NO**

   Why? _____

   Think: What do you think food coloring is mostly made of? _____

5. Name a mixture you have made at home. _____

   What ingredients did you use? _____

   _____

   _____

   What did you do with the mixture you made? _____

   _____

   _____

SCIENTIFIC METHOD REVIEW—MORE MIXTURES

Share your journal entries, documents, and experiences working with mixtures with your class in a discussion moderated by your teacher.

WORKING WITH EMULSIONS

Directions: Work in pairs to explore how to add an **emulsifier** to blend a mixture.

Emulsion—the combination of two liquids that do not mix, like oil and water or oil and vinegar
Emulsifier—an added ingredient that allows ingredients in a mixture to blend for a short time.
Add mustard to oil and vinegar and you will create salad dressing that stays blended for a while.

TEAM MATERIALS

- bottles from Activity 2
- colored pencils
- cooking oil
- dish soap (Dawn® or Joy®)
- eyedroppers
- food coloring–various colors
- funnels
- measuring cups
- permanent markers
- timers or stopwatches
- warm or hot water

GETTING STARTED—BLENDING AN EMULSION

1. Carefully place your mixture from Activity 2 on the table. Try not to shake up the layers in the **emulsion** in the bottle.

2. Use colored pencils to sketch and label the settled emulsion in the box on the right. Describe what you see.

_____

_____

3. Measure out 1 ounce of dish soap and use a funnel to pour it into the bottle.

4. Watch the soap and the oil interact. What happens when you add the dish soap?

_____

_____

5. Measure out 1 ounce of warm or hot water into a cup. Use a funnel to *slowly* add the water to the mixture.

6. Sketch this interaction in the box on the right. Describe how the soap, oil, and warm or hot water interact.

_____

_____

_____

_____

SETTLED EMULSION

SOAP, OIL, HOT WATER

 NAME _____

WORKING WITH EMULSIONS

Directions: Work in pairs and continue working with your emulsions. Read all the directions before beginning each activity so you know when you need to stop and start the timers.

SHAKE IT!

1. Make sure the cap is secure on your mixture. Shake the bottle for 15 seconds.

2. Set the timer to see how long the mixture takes to settle. Stop the timer when the emulsion has settled (approximately 3 minutes).

   TOTAL TIME: _____

3. While you wait, describe the reaction when the bottle was shaken. How did the mixture look right after being shaken up? _____

   _____

4. Add two more color drops to the settled solution and set the timer. Time how long the food coloring takes to get through the oil. (Stretch while you wait, but keep your eyes on the drops!)

   TOTAL TIME: _____

5. Describe the results. _____

   _____

ADDING WARM WATER

1. Add 3 ounces of warm water to the settled emulsion. Describe what happens. _____

   _____

2. Add one more drop of food coloring, and put the cap back on tightly.

3. Wait 3 minutes. Stretch. Describe and sketch the results in the space below.

4. Save the emulsion to use again in Activity 4. Figure out a safe way to store the bottles.

_____

_____

_____

_____

_____

★ ★ ADD A NEW LABEL TO THE BOTTLE—"EMULSION ACTIVITIES 2 AND 3." ★ ★

WORKING WITH EMULSIONS

JOURNAL ENTRY

1. Name foods or drinks you have tried that are **solutions**. List the ingredients you know that are in each solution.

   FOOD: _____

   INGREDIENTS: _____

   _____

   DRINK: _____

   INGREDIENTS: _____

   _____

2. All of the following foods are **emulsions**. Check the ones you have eaten or drunk.

   ☐ butter   ☐ margarine   ☐ salad dressing

   ☐ ice cream   ☐ milk   ☐ whipped cream

3. Can you explain why salad dressing in bottles often has layers? Use words from this unit's vocabulary to help you explain.

   _____

   _____

4. If you added salt to a glass of water, what would you make?

   ### A SOLUTION   AN EMULSION

   Explain your reasoning. _____

   _____

5. Explain how an **emulsifier** works. _____

   _____

   _____

SCIENTIFIC METHOD REVIEW—WORKING WITH EMULSIONS

Share your journal entries, documents, and experiences with emulsions with your class in a discussion moderated by your teacher.

ADDING TO EMULSIONS

Directions: Work in pairs with mixtures and emulsions. Read through the directions before beginning so you will know when you need to stop and start the timers.

TEAM MATERIALS

- baby oil
- baking soda
- bottle from Activity 2 and 3
- colored pencils
- funnels
- measuring cups
- plastic spoons
- rock salt
- rubbing alcohol
- small, clear cups
- table salt
- timers
- trays or tubs
- vinegar
- warm water

GETTING STARTED—OBSERVE THE EMULSION

1. Carefully study your emulsion bottle. It should be settled in a number of layers.

2. Sketch the unshaken emulsion in the box on the right and label the layers.

ADDING BABY OIL TO THE EMULSION

1. The cooking oil should be settled at the top of your emulsion. Measure out 1 ounce of baby oil. Use a funnel to add the baby oil to the emulsion.

2. Wait for it to settle. (Stretch or run in place.)

3. Observe the reaction. Which oil settles on top?

COOKING OIL   BABY OIL

Why do you think that this oil settled on the top?

_____

_____

Which oil appears to be denser?

COOKING OIL   BABY OIL

4. Sketch the new emulsion in the bottle on the right and label the layers.

5. Measure out 3 ounces of warm water. Use a funnel to pour this water into the bottle. Put the cap on the bottle, and shake it vigorously for 15 seconds.

6. Describe the results of the reaction.

_____

_____

SETTLED EMULSION

ADDING BABY OIL

ADDING TO EMULSIONS

ADDING TABLE SALT AND ROCK SALT

1. Carefully add a spoonful of table salt to the settled emulsion. Does the salt stay on top of the oil?

   YES   NO

2. Observe the movement of the table salt. Does it float through the oil to the water, or does it sink quickly?

   FLOAT   SINK

3. Sketch the traveling salt in the box on the right.

4. Carefully add $\frac{1}{2}$ a teaspoon of rock salt to the emulsion. (Rock or flake salts have larger pieces.) Describe what the larger pieces of salt do.

   _____

   _____

5. Shake the emulsion. Observe the large salt pieces in the emulsion. Sketch your observation on the right.

ADDING RUBBING ALCOHOL

1. Measure out 1 ounce of rubbing alcohol. Use a funnel to slowly add the rubbing alcohol to the emulsion.

2. Describe the reaction of the other materials with the rubbing alcohol.

   _____

   _____

3. Set the timer. Shake the emulsion several times until all of the ingredients are mixed again. How long did it take?

   ☐ **15 SECONDS**

   ☐ **30 SECONDS**

   ☐ **45 SECONDS**

   ☐ **LONGER**

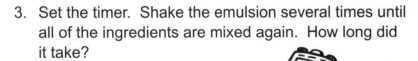

4. Observe how the materials settle this time.

5. Use your colored pencils to sketch the settled rubbing alcohol emulsion. Label each layer.

TABLE SALT

ROCK SALT

RUBBING ALCOHOL EMULSION

NAME _____

ADDING TO EMULSIONS

BAKING SODA AND VINEGAR

Note: Follow these directions exactly. If weather permits, it is best to do this activity outside. Either way, place the bottle in a tub or tray.

1. Put one teaspoon of baking soda into a cup. In chemistry, baking soda is called a *base*.

2. Take the cap off your emulsion.

3. Pour 1-ounce of vinegar into the cup. Vinegar is an *acid*.

4. Use a funnel to pour the combination of vinegar and baking soda into your bottle and put the cap on securely. The material will start fizzing right away, so pour quickly and carefully.

5. Describe the reaction within your emulsion. _____

_____

_____

6. Use colored pencils to illustrate the reaction below.

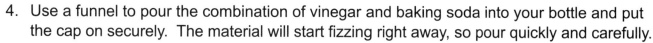

VINEGAR & BAKING SODA EMULSION

ADDING TO EMULSIONS

JOURNAL ENTRY

1. List at least 3 scientific facts about chemistry, emulsions, or mixtures that you learned by doing today's activities.

   Fact 1: _____

   _____

   Fact 2: _____

   _____

   Fact 3: _____

   _____

2. Why is it useful to use colored pencils to sketch the results of chemistry experiments?

   _____

3. Why did the oil not stay fully mixed with the water? _____

   _____

4. Which of the following materials will not mix with the others? Circle your answers.

   FOOD COLORING   **SALT**   **WATER**   **BABY OIL**   **SUGAR**

   Why? _____

   _____

5. Are you creating a solution, a mixture, or an emulsion when you mix oil, water, and dish soap together?

   A SOLUTION   **A MIXTURE**   **AN EMULSION**

   How can you tell? _____

   _____

   _____

SCIENTIFIC METHOD REVIEW—ADDING TO EMULSIONS

Gather with your teacher and class. Take turns sharing your journal entries, questions, and experiences with emulsions.

CHALLENGE: BE A CHEMIST: USE THE SCIENTIFIC METHOD

TEACHER NOTES

—Circulate during the period, enforcing the restrictions on materials and the amounts used. If the weather is favorable, you may wish to do this activity outside.

—Remind student teams that they must clean up as they complete each project.

EQUIPMENT

- ☐ 6-ounce, clear cups
- ☐ large, clear plastic bottles with caps
- ☐ colored pencils
- ☐ eyedroppers (if needed)
- ☐ funnels
- ☐ paper towels
- ☐ small plastic spoons
- ☐ trays or tubs

ACCEPTABLE MATERIALS

You may not use more than 2 ounces of each of these materials.

- ☐ baby oil
- ☐ cooking oil
- ☐ corn syrup
- ☐ dish soap
- ☐ flour
- ☐ food coloring—any colors; liquid or powder
- ☐ granulated sugar or cubes
- ☐ laundry soap—any variety; liquid or powder
- ☐ olive oil
- ☐ pepper
- ☐ salt
- ☐ rock salt or flaked salt

MATERIALS WITH SPECIAL AMOUNTS

- ☐ 1 teaspoon baking soda
- ☐ 1 ounce rubbing alcohol
- ☐ 1 ounce vinegar
- ☐ water—hot, warm, cool, or ice not more than half the bottle

CHALLENGE: BE A CHEMIST: USE THE SCIENTIFIC METHOD

Directions: Now you and your partner get to create a mix of ingredients of your own with the materials provided using the Scientific Method. This method is similar to the Design Process used by engineers when they design and build. Discuss the similarities with your partner.

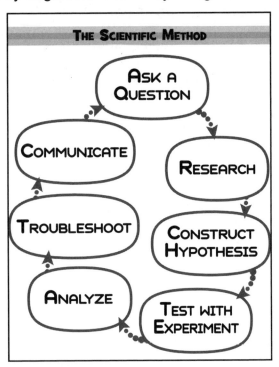

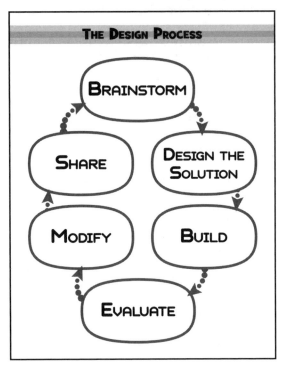

REMINDER: Keep in mind the measuring and pouring skills you have practiced and the tools you can use. Remember to record amounts and reactions when creating your mixtures.

ASK A QUESTION—WHAT DO YOU WANT TO TEST? Think of the materials you have already used and how they mixed together.

What would you like to mix together now? _____

Do you want to make a *solution*, a *mixture*, or an *emulsion*? _____

Will you add an emulsifier? **YES** **NO**

If yes, which one? _____

RESEARCH: What do you want to find out? What research do you need to do before beginning?

_____

CONSTRUCT A HYPOTHESIS: Describe what you think will happen.

_____

_____

CHALLENGE: BE A CHEMIST: USE THE SCIENTIFIC METHOD

TEST THROUGH EXPERIMENTATION

On the chart, list up to five ingredients you will use to start. You will be able to add two more ingredients later, if you wish. Remember to pay attention to the amounts allowed on the master list. Record the amounts you used.

SOLUTION, MIXTURE, OR EMULSION	
MATERIALS	AMOUNTS
1.	
2.	
3.	
4.	
5.	
6.	
7.	

☐ Use the chart on page 84 to record the reaction of each ingredient as you add it.

☐ Label your ingredients and note whether you shake the mixture or not each time.

☐ Note other reactions that occur.

REMINDER: NO TEAM SHOULD FINISH THE LAB WORK AND REPORT IN LESS THAN 15 MINUTES.

CHALLENGE: BE A CHEMIST: USE THE SCIENTIFIC METHOD

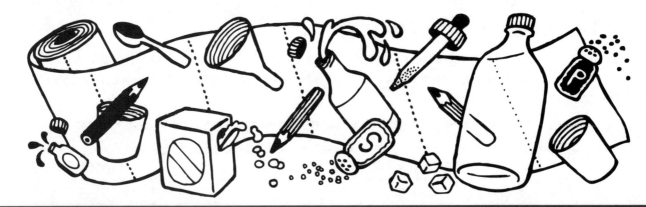

PROCEDURE—STEP-BY-STEP			
INGREDIENT	AMOUNT USED	SHAKEN	REACTION
1.		YES NO	
2.		YES NO	
3.		YES NO	
4.		YES NO	
5.		YES NO	
6.		YES NO	
7.		YES NO	

CHALLENGE: BE A CHEMIST: USE THE SCIENTIFIC METHOD

ANALYZE: Did you succeed in making the type of mixture you had planned?   **YES   NO**

Explain: _____

_____

After your ingredients settled, what did you see? _____

_____

What did your ingredients create?   **SOLUTION   MIXTURE   EMULSION**

Add one or two more ingredients. Include them in the list on the previous page. What did you add and why?

_____

_____

TROUBLESHOOT: If you could do anything differently, what would you change?

_____

_____

COMMUNICATE RESULTS: What happened with your ingredients? _____

_____

Which ingredients had the most interesting reactions? _____

_____

What did you learn about solutions, mixtures, and emulsions? _____

_____

Sketch your final solution, mixture, or emulsion in the space on the right, and label the ingredient layers (if they are visible).

Do you think you were successful?   **YES   NO**

Why? _____

_____

_____

AIR IN ACTION

4 sessions: 1 session for each activity (approximately 1 to $1\frac{1}{2}$ hours per session)

Focus: Physical Science, Physics—properties of air, air in motion

CONNECTIONS AND SUGGESTIONS

SCIENCE—Students will explore some of the properties of air—air takes up space, air can be moved and manipulated, and air has mass and weight.

Students will also work with the concept of gravity as they fly their helicopter models and launch their parachutes. The helicopters are designed to show students how the presence of air affects objects moving through it and how air can be manipulated by moving objects such as rotor blades. The parachute and helicopter movements are both effective because air has mass and density and both can be manipulated to do work.

Air can also be manipulated to move faster when compressed. Balloon rockets use compressed air to carry a small rocket (balloon) across a room or from the floor to the ceiling.

TECHNOLOGY—Students may use computers, tablets, cameras and/or video equipment to record their observations of actions and reactions as they build and launch a variety of flying vehicles. They may wish to use technology to describe the problems encountered, the solutions attempted, and the success rate of each activity.

ENGINEERING—Aeronautics is a division of engineering devoted to the study of travel through air. Students will be using specific materials and tools during the design process in order to construct parachutes, helicopters, and balloon rockets. They will attempt to create more effective and efficient designs and design and plan simple experiments to test their creations.

MATH—Students will make accurate measurements of length using appropriate tools. They will be directed to use specific measurements to make a variety of models. They will be recording the results of different experiments in terms of distances traveled (linear measurement), weights used, and direction of rotation.

DISCUSSION PROMPT: How do you explain air?

You can't usually see air, touch it, or taste it, but you know it is there. Air surrounds us. We breathe in air to live. Some days you can feel a breeze or see the wind blow leaves around. That is air moving. We use air to do many things such as pump up tires, blow up balloons, cool ourselves off, and fly kites. Helicopters, jets, rockets, and other flying vehicles use air, too.

AIR IN ACTION

UNIT MATERIALS (for a class of 30 to 35)

- ☐ fabric (to make squares 10" or larger)
- ☐ plastic shopping bags (to make squares 10" or larger)
- ☐ balloons—round, long, small, and large
- ☐ clear tape and masking tape
- ☐ construction paper
- ☐ copy paper
- ☐ fishing line (8-pound test or higher)
- ☐ heavy paper—index cards or file folders
- ☐ hole punches
- ☐ markers
- ☐ measuring tapes
- ☐ paper clips—large and small
- ☐ push pins
- ☐ rulers
- ☐ scissors
- ☐ small toys or plastic people
- ☐ straight straws (large)
- ☐ string, twine, or yarn
- ☐ timers or stopwatches

NOTES

_____

_____

_____

_____

_____

_____

_____

_____

_____

_____

_____

_____

_____

FIND OUT MORE

A Force Is a Push or a Pull

This short clip explains the term *force* and demonstrates with a balloon rocket.

https://www.youtube.com/watch?v=_LdcxCdB-s8

Exploratorium (San Francisco)—Rotor Copter

http://www.exploratorium.edu/science_explorer/roto-copter

Explain That Stuff—Helicopters

http://www.explainthatstuff.com/helicopter.html

Safety Note: All websites should be checked prior to student viewing to be certain that content is appropriate.

AIR IN ACTION VOCABULARY

<u>aeronautics</u>—field of engineering that studies flight

<u>ascend</u>—to go up

<u>canopy</u>—fabric part of a parachute

<u>descend</u>—to move down

<u>efficient</u>—working in a well-organized way

<u>gravity</u>—the force that attracts things to the center of the earth

<u>launch</u>—to set in motion; to place an object into the air so that it can go up, or in water so that it can move forward

<u>propel</u>—to cause to move, usually forward

<u>reverse</u>—to switch directions and go the opposite way

<u>rotate</u>—to move in a circular pattern

<u>rotor</u>—the rotating component of a motor or a machine

<u>rotor blade</u>—a blade attached to the rotor which rotates clockwise or counterclockwise

<u>template</u>—a pattern or blueprint

<u>twirl</u>—to turn in a circle; to spin in a circle

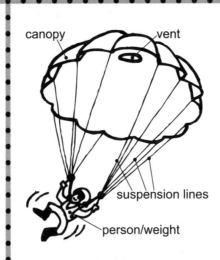

Helicopter

Parachute

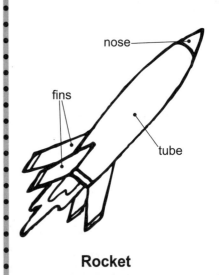

Rocket

AIR IN ACTION

WHO KNEW?

HELICOPTERS

HELICOPTERS

How do helicopters fly? Helicopters have rotor blades instead of wings. Rotor blades are rounded on top and flat on the bottom. This shape helps them catch air to lift the helicopter up.

The rotor blades are attached to a rotor. The rotor is part of the motor. The motor makes the rotor blades spin around. Helicopters often have large blades on the top and smaller ones on the tail.

When air comes into contact with an object, it flows around the object it hits and creates a force that can lift the object. To take off, the rotor spins the blades, and the helicopter goes straight up in the air. It does not need a long runway, like an airplane does. A helicopter can go forward, and it can go backward. It can go sideways, too. A helicopter can even stay in one place up in the air! This is called *hovering*.

Helicopters do not need much room to land, either. They just drop straight down. This makes it easy for them to land in small places like parking lots, fields, and rooftops.

Have you ever ridden in a helicopter?   **YES   NO**

If you have, what was it like? What did you see? _____

_____

If not, where would you like to go in a helicopter? _____

What would you like to see? _____

Think about the times you have seen helicopters flying. Can you name a few ways helicopters are used? Brainstorm with your classmates.

1. _____

2. _____

3. _____

4. _____

AIR IN ACTION

AIR AT WORK

Air works in many different ways. It can help birds glide as they search for food. Gentle breezes can cool us down in hot weather. Wind can make power for our homes. It also helps kites fly.

Air helps planes, jets, and helicopters stay up in the sky and fly to faraway places.

When air fills a parachute, the parachute slows down. Without a parachute, gravity would make the person or thing drop too quickly. Air lets the person or thing attached to the parachute float down gently.

What happens if you blow up a balloon and let go before you tie the end? The air rushes out and the balloon takes off! The air **propels** the balloon forward.

1. Think about your five senses. When might you be able to detect air using each one? Answer in complete sentences.

   SIGHT— _____

   _____

   HEARING— _____

   _____

   TOUCH— _____

   _____

   TASTE— _____

   _____

   SMELL— _____

2. Brainstorm some things you can do that require air.

   _____   _____

   _____   _____

   _____   _____

MAKING HELICOPTERS

Directions: Work in pairs to make and test helicopters. Each partner will make his or her own helicopter. You will partner up to observe and to time the flights of each other's helicopters.

TEAM MATERIALS
- clear tape or masking tape
- large paper clips
- small paper clips
- markers
- paper
- rulers
- scissors
- timers or stopwatches

HELICOPTER 1 DESIGN

Your first helicopter template will look like this:

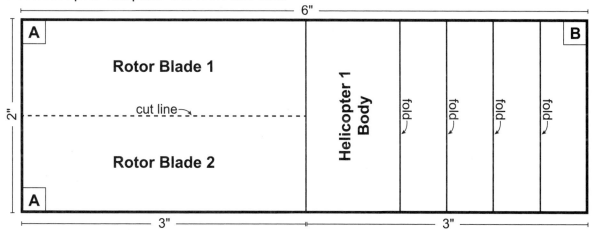

HELICOPTER 1—ROTOR BLADES

1. Use a ruler to measure a strip of paper that is 6" long and 2" wide. Cut out this 6" × 2" strip.

2. Draw a 2" line across the middle of the paper strip creating two equal halves. Label the halves **A** and **B**. Side **A** will be for the rotor blades, and side **B** will be for the body of the helicopter.

3. Use a ruler to draw a 3" line dividing side **A** in half lengthwise. Use scissors to cut along the 3" line on one side. You have now created the two rotor blades for your helicopter. Label them **Rotor Blade 1** and **Rotor Blade 2**.

HELICOPTER 1—BODY

4. Now work on side **B**—the body of the helicopter. Use a ruler to measure four lines, each $\frac{1}{2}$ inch apart.

5. On side **B**, fold the paper at each of the 4 lines you drew, rolling it up as you do go.

6. Use a small paper clip to hold the 4 folds in place.

7. Fold the rotor blades over on each side of the folded **B** section. (They won't stay up, but the folds on each side are needed for the rotor blades to work.)

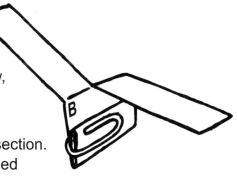

★ ★ ★ SAVE HELICOPTER 1 ★ ★ ★

 _____

MAKING HELICOPTERS

FLYING HELICOPTER 1

1. Hold the tips of the two rotor blades between your fingers.

2. Raise your hand as high as you can and let go of the rotor blades. (If the model was made correctly, the rotor blades will twirl, and the helicopter will gradually descend to the floor.)

   Safety Note: Try to find a sturdy box, chair, or table to stand on safely. Make certain you have teacher approval for your choice of launch area.

3. Launch the helicopter several times to get acquainted with the process. Rotor Blade 1 should be facing you.

4. In which direction is your helicopter rotating?

   ### CLOCKWISE   COUNTERCLOCKWISE

REVERSING THE ROTOR BLADES

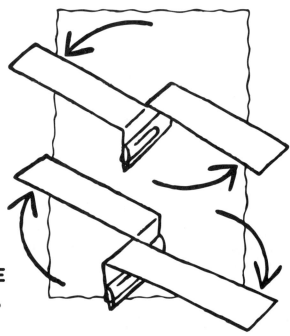

1. Reverse the folds of the two rotor blades. Rotor 1 will still be facing you when you launch. The rotor that was forward is now to the rear. The rotor blade that was to the rear is now forward.

2. Again, raise your hand as high as you can. Let go of the rotor blades.

3. Observe the direction the model is turning or whirling in. Which direction is it going in now?

   ### CLOCKWISE   COUNTERCLOCKWISE

4. Did the helicopter rotor blades switch directions?

   ### YES   NO

   Why or why not? _____

   _____

   _____

★ ★ ★ SAVE HELICOPTER 1 ★ ★ ★

MAKING HELICOPTERS

Directions: Use the template on page 94 as a guide (or a pattern) to help you make helicopter 2.

HELICOPTER 2 DESIGN

HELICOPTER 2—ROTOR BLADES

1. Use a ruler to measure a strip of paper that is 8" long and 3" wide. Cut out the 8" × 3" strip.
2. Measure 4" down the length of the strip on each side and make dots. Then, draw a line across the paper, connecting the dots to divide the strip in half.
3. Mark one half of the strip **A** and the other half **B**. Side **A** will be for the rotor blades, and side **B** will be for the body of the helicopter.
4. Make a dot in the middle of the 3" edge of side **A** by measuring in $1\frac{1}{2}$" from the 8" edge.
5. Draw a straight line from the dot to the dividing line you drew at the 4" mark. This line should divide side **A** in half, lengthwise.
6. Cut along the line you just drew on side **A** to make the two rotor blades. Label the rotor blades **Rotor Blade 1** and **Rotor Blade 2**.

HELICOPTER 2—BODY

1. Divide side **B** in half. Measure 2" in from the 3" edge and make a pencil mark on the outside edge of both sides. Draw a straight line connecting these 2 points. This should divide side **B** in half, widthwise. (See Diagram 1 on page 94.)
2. Divide this line into 3 equal sections by making a dot at 1" in from the end of the line on each side of the paper. (See Diagram 1 on page 94.)
3. Cut in 1" on each side of the line. Do not cut the middle 1-inch section. (See Diagram 1 on page 94.)
4. Fold each cut section over the center. This should form a rectangle.
5. Take one corner of the very bottom of this folded rectangle and fold it up to form a triangle overlapping the rest of this piece. (See Diagram 2 on page 94.) Hold the fold in place by putting a small piece of clear tape over this end.

TEST IT

1. Fold one rotor blade back and the other rotor blade forward as you did in the first model.
2. Hold the model as high as you can by the tips of the rotor blades and then let go.

   Describe what happened. _____

_____

★ ★ ★ SAVE HELICOPTER 2 ★ ★ ★

MAKING HELICOPTERS

MAKING HELICOPTER 2

Your second helicopter template will look like this:

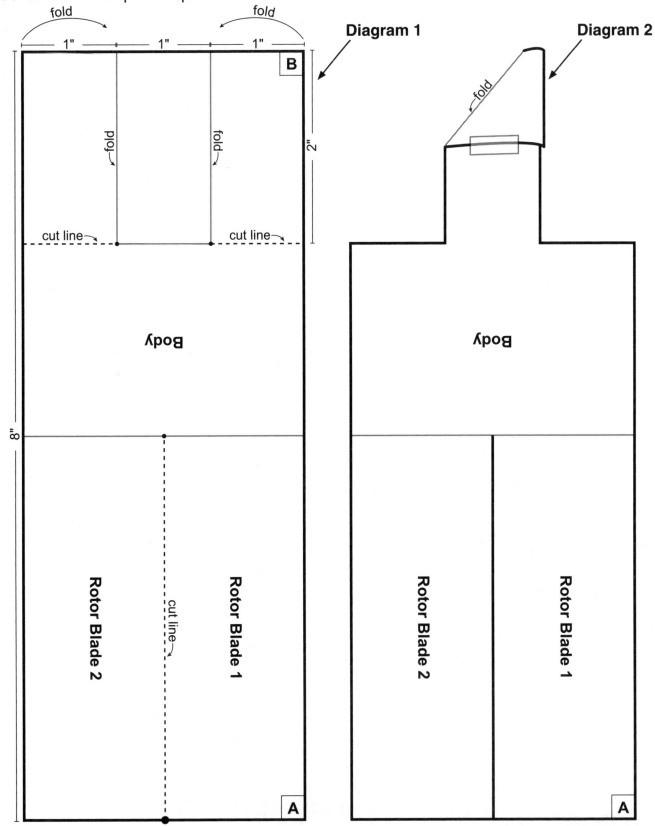

MAKING HELICOPTERS

DESIGN YOUR OWN HELICOPTER

1. Think about a helicopter you would like to make. You could make it bigger, smaller, wider, or shorter than the first two you made. Consider one of the following variations, or one of your own:
   - different lengths or widths for the rotor blades
   - three or four rotor blades instead of two
   - a different body shape
   - more weights or a different type of weight

2. Draw a pattern and describe your design.

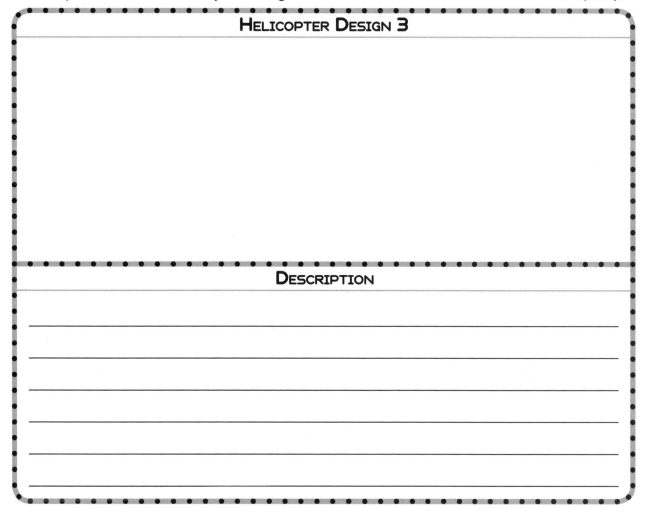

HELICOPTER DESIGN 3

DESCRIPTION

_____

_____

_____

_____

_____

_____

3. Build your helicopter.

4. Test your helicopter, and make adjustments as needed. Explain the adjustments you made.

_____

_____

MAKING HELICOPTERS

DESIGN YOUR OWN HELICOPTER

ADD WEIGHT TO HELICOPTER DESIGN 3

1. Add a small paper clip to the tip (body) of your design and fly the helicopter again.

   Did it twirl faster with the extra weight?   **YES   NO**

2. Replace the small paper clip with a large paper clip. Fly the helicopter again.

   What did you observe? _____

   _____

3. Try using a second large paper clip placed across the first one to form an X. Retest your helicopter and describe your results.

   _____

   _____

4. Add a third large paper clip attached to the center of the craft or to the bottom landing gear. Does the helicopter still twirl?

   YES   NO

   What did you observe? _____

   _____

TIME THE FLIGHTS

1. Work with your partner. Take turns timing your three helicopters from launch to landing.
2. Try to do two test flights for each model.
3. Record your flight times below.

	FLIGHT 1	FLIGHT 2
DESIGN 1		
DESIGN 2		
DESIGN 3		

★ ★ ★ SAVE HELICOPTER 3 ★ ★ ★

MAKING HELICOPTERS

HELICOPTER FUN!

REVERSE THE ROTOR BLADES

1. Drop the last helicopter you made to see which way it turns.

   CLOCKWISE   COUNTERCLOCKWISE

2. Now reverse the direction of the rotor blades. To do this, fold each **rotor blade** back in the opposite direction. Make sure the new folds have sharp creases.

3. Try it out again—drop the helicopter from as high as you can reach. Which direction did the rotor blades turn this time?

   CLOCKWISE   COUNTERCLOCKWISE

4. What happened to the direction in which the helicopter was rotating?

   _____

   _____

ADD COLOR TO THE ROTOR BLADES

1. Use markers to color the rotor blades. Try red on **Rotor Blade 1** and blue on **Rotor Blade 2**. Use green and yellow on the reverse sides.

2. Retest your helicopter with these colors.

3. Describe the colors in motion. _____

   _____

4. Reverse the rotor blades. Describe these colors in motion. _____

   _____

5. Try these combinations or other designs if time allows.

A	B
red	blue

A	B
green	yellow

A	B

NAME _____

MAKING HELICOPTERS

JOURNAL ENTRY

1. Explain how air helps a helicopter fly. _____

   _____

   _____

2. What do the rotor blades do? _____

   _____

   _____

3. What variables did you change to create your third helicopter design? _____

   _____

   _____

   Explain how these variables affected the flight of the helicopter. _____

   _____

   _____

4. Which helicopter design worked the best?   **1   2   3**

   Why? _____

   _____

   _____

5. What was the most important factor in making the helicopter work?

   SIZE   WEIGHT   DESIGN

   Why? _____

   _____

   _____

DESIGN PROCESS REVIEW—MAKING HELICOPTERS

Share your responses, documents, and experiences making helicopters in a class discussion led by your teacher. Demonstrate your helicopter models if time allows.

MAKING PARACHUTES

Directions: Work in pairs to make and test parachutes. Each student will make his or her own parachute. You will partner up to observe and to time the flights of each other's parachutes.

TEAM MATERIALS

- clear tape
- fabric (to make squares 10" or larger)
- fishing line (8-lb. test or higher)
- hole punches
- large paper clips
- masking tape
- paper—different types

- plastic shopping bags (to make squares 10" or larger)
- rulers
- scissors
- string and yarn
- *optional:* table, chair, or small ladder for launching; small toys or plastic people

NOTE: If possible, provide students with the option to use string, yarn, or fishing line for parachutes.

MAKING PARACHUTE 1—PREPARE THE CHUTE

1.	Carefully measure a piece of paper to create a 5" square. Then, cut the square out.	2.	Fold the 5" square in half. Fold the paper in half again to divide it into equal quarters.
3.	Look at the creases in the paper. Three of the creases are bent in one direction and one in another direction. Refold the last crease so that all creases fold in the same direction.	4.	Place dots about $\frac{3}{4}$" in diagonally from each corner.
5.	Fold a piece of tape over each corner (on both sides) in order to make the corners more durable.	6.	Use a hole punch to make holes through the tape-covered paper where you marked the corners earlier.

NAME

MAKING PARACHUTES

COMPLETING PARACHUTE 1—ATTACHING THE LINES

1. Cut four 12-inch pieces of string, yarn, or fishing line. *Perhaps you and your partner(s) can each use a different type to compare.*

2. Tie one 12-inch line through each taped hole in the paper and secure the line with a double knot. Check that all the knots are tight.

3. Hold all four lines in one hand. Tie them together as far away from the parachute as possible. (Try to have at least 8" of string between the knots on the corners of the parachute and the knot connecting the four strings.)

4. Attach a paper clip to the knot that is holding the four strings of the parachute. Tie the ends of the strings around the clip or poke the paper clip through the knot.

TESTING PARACHUTE 1

1. Hold the parachute as high as you can and let go. It should float gently toward the floor.

2. Pick up the chute. Check the knots to make sure they are tight.

3. Toss the parachute into the air. It should straighten out and float down again. Does it float gently?

YES   NO

Explain. _____

_____

_____

4. Add a second paper clip to the parachute and launch the parachute. How does the parachute fly with more weight added?

_____

_____

_____

5. **With adult supervision,** try standing on a chair or desk to launch the parachute again. How did it fly from a higher launch?

_____

_____

MAKING PARACHUTES

Directions: Make larger parachutes by using the same design. Use the same type of paper, or try one of a different weight such as newsprint.

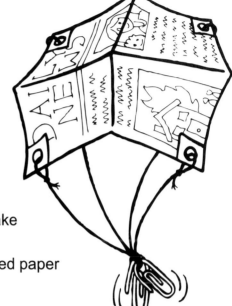

MAKING PARACHUTE 2

1. Carefully measure and cut a piece of paper to create a 12" square.

2. Fold the 12" square in half. Fold the paper in half again to divide it into four equal quarters.

3. Look at the creases in the paper. Three of the folds are going in one direction and one in another. Refold the last fold so that all creases fold in the same direction.

4. Draw dots in about $\frac{3}{4}$" diagonally from each corner.

5. Fold a piece of tape over each corner (both sides) to make the corners more durable.

6. Use a hole punch to make holes through the tape-covered paper where you marked the corners earlier.

COMPLETING PARACHUTE 2

1. Cut four 12-inch pieces of fishing line, string, yarn or twine. *Perhaps you and your partner can each use a different type to compare.*

2. Tie a 12-inch line through each hole in the paper and secure each line with a double knot. Check that all the knots are tight.

3. Hold all four lines and tie them together as far away from the paper parachute as possible. (Try to have at least 6" of string between the two sets of knots.)

4. Use paper clips as weights. Start with one and add more as needed after testing.

TESTING THE PARACHUTE

1. Hold the parachute as high as you can and let go. It should float gently toward the floor.

2. Try tossing the parachute into the air. It should straighten out and float down again.

   Does it float gently?   **YES   NO**

   Explain. _____

3. Add a second paper clip to the parachute and launch the parachute. How does the parachute fly with more weight added?

   _____

   _____

   _____

MAKING PARACHUTES

Directions: This time, use the same design but a different material. Use a square cut from a plastic bag or fabric.

MAKING PARACHUTE 3

1. Measure a 10" or 12" square of fabric or plastic (shopping bag) to use for this parachute.
2. Draw dots about $\frac{3}{4}$" in—diagonally from each corner.
3. Fold a piece of tape over each corner (both sides) to make the corners more durable.
4. Use a hole punch to make holes through the tape-covered material where you marked the corners earlier.

COMPLETING PARACHUTE 3

1. Tie 12" to 18" pieces of fishing line or string to each of the four corners of the square. Check that all knots are tight.
2. Hold all four lines together and tie them as far away from the parachute as possible. Try to have at least 9" of string between the knots and where the strings are tied together.
3. Create a weight using paper clips, small toys, or plastic people.

TESTING THE PARACHUTE

1. Hold the parachute as high as you can and let go. It should float gently toward the floor.
2. Try tossing the parachute into the air. It should straighten out and float down again.

   Does it float gently?   **YES   NO**

   Explain. _____

   _____

3. With adult supervision, climb onto a table, chair, or small ladder and drop the parachute. You can do this test outside by tossing it as high as you can up into the air—away from trees and the roof.
4. It can take several trials to get the parachute to gracefully unfold and fall. It also takes several trials to determine what kind of weight works best and how heavy to make it. What worked?

   _____

   _____

5. Add a second paper clip (or some other weight) to the parachute and launch it. How does the parachute fly with more weight added?

   _____

   _____

 _____

MAKING PARACHUTES

DESIGN YOUR OWN PARACHUTE

1. Try a different size or variation for this parachute design. Make it bigger, smaller, wider, or shorter or try another variation. Here are some suggestions:
   - a different type of paper, plastic bag, or fabric
   - different lengths for the suspension strings
   - different weights—multiple paper clips, washers, toy people, etc.
   - a different canopy shape—circle, rectangle, triangle, or make a double canopy
   - a hole or vent at the top of the canopy

2. Draw and describe your design and show the measurements. List the materials you will use.

PARACHUTE DESIGN 4	DESCRIPTION
	_____
	_____
	_____
	_____
	MATERIALS
	_____ _____ _____
	_____ _____ _____

3. Build your parachute.
4. Test your parachute and make adjustments as needed.

TIME THE LAUNCHES

1. Work with your partner.
2. Take turns timing *each* of your parachutes from launch to landing. If possible, have another person film your launches to review and discuss later.
3. Record your times and observations in the chart below.

PARACHUTE	TIME	OBSERVATIONS
SMALL PAPER PARACHUTE 1		
LARGE PAPER PARACHUTE 2		
FABRIC/PLASTIC PARACHUTE 3		
PERSONAL DESIGN PARACHUTE 4		

 NAME _____

MAKING PARACHUTES

JOURNAL ENTRY

1. Which material do you think worked the best for the parachute? _____

   _____

   Why? _____

   _____

   _____

2. Which type of material worked best for the suspension strings? _____

   _____

   Why? _____

   _____

3. What did you discover about weights when testing your parachutes? _____

   _____

   _____

4. Describe the best method to launch a parachute. _____

   _____

5. Describe and sketch one more parachute you
   would like to make in the box to the right.

   _____

   _____

   _____

   _____

   _____

DESIGN PROCESS REVIEW—MAKING PARACHUTES

Share your responses, documents, and experiences making parachutes with your classmates in a class discussion led by your teacher. Demonstrate your parachutes if time allows.

MAKING BALLOON ROCKETS

Directions: Read both pages of this activity before beginning so that you will be prepared. You will need to work in teams of four to create and launch the balloon rockets. The launch goes very fast, and every team member will need to be prepared to do his or her job in a short amount of time.

TEAM MATERIALS

- balloons of several sizes and shapes (long, round, etc.)
- clear tape or masking tape
- fishing line (8-lb. test or higher)
- heavy paper
- large, straight straws
- markers

- measuring tapes
- push pins
- rulers
- scissors
- timer
- *optional:* balloon pump

TEACHER PREPARATION

1. Establish launching areas and rules for the Rocket Launch Zones. You will need at least 5 Rocket Launch Zones to accommodate a class of students working in teams of four. These zones can be set up outdoors if the weather is cooperative and space is available. Students will need to use pushpins in the walls, trees, or other surfaces.

TEAM PREPARATION—THE ROCKET LAUNCH ZONE

1. First, measure up about 4 feet from the ground on a sturdy pole, tree, bulletin board, or wall, and mark the spot. Tie one end of the fishing line to the needle end of the pushpin, and stick the pin in the marked spot.

2. Measure out approximately 30 feet of the fishing line from the pushpin. The path from one end of the line to the place where it is attached should be a clear, straight line with no obstructions.

3. Place the unattached end of the fishing line where it can be reached when needed. After the team has measured and assembled its launch line together, each member will choose a different task in order to assist with the launch.

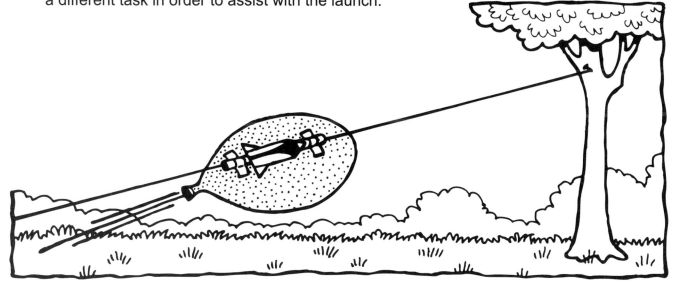

MAKING BALLOON ROCKETS

THE BALLOON ROCKET—PREP AND LAUNCH!

Teammate 1 will be in charge of making the paper rocket shape and later documenting the launch of the balloon rocket. Use an index card or a piece of file folder and markers to create a long, thin rocket. It should not be more than 2" wide and should be shorter than the straw. Color the rocket if time allows.

Teammate 2 will be in charge of taping the rocket to the straw. If it's a flex straw, cut off the flex end. Slip the end of the fishing line through the straw. Make sure the rocket is pointing in the direction in which it will be launched. You will need to hold the line taut when the time comes to launch.

Teammate 3 will blow up a balloon and hold the end tightly. Do not put a knot at the end. Hold the balloon carefully under the straw so that the tape can be attached. The rocket will be on top of the straw and the balloon underneath. Do not let air out of the balloon until you are ready to launch.

Teammate 4 will need to prepare three or four tape strips while the balloon is being blown up. This way, both hands will be free to attach the tape to the balloon when the time comes. Tape the balloon to the straw in two places.

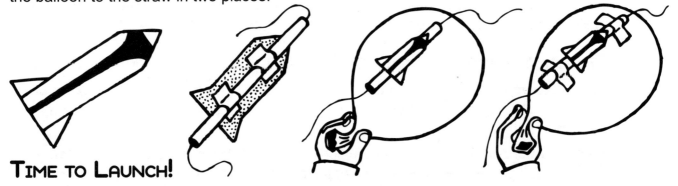

TIME TO LAUNCH!

Teammate 1 documents the launch, and after, measures the distance traveled.

Teammate 2 holds the fishing line taut for the entire launch. Make sure the fishing line is lined up with the center of the straw and that you are standing in a straight line from the point where the fishing line is attached. This way the line will have the least friction and will not slow the "rocket" down.

Teammate 3 blows up the balloon, holds it closed until the 3-count to launch time, and then lets go!

Teammate 4 counts down to launch—**3, 2, 1** and let go!

REVIEWING THE LAUNCH

1. Describe the launch of your rocket. Did it go smoothly, or did you have problems?

2. Did the balloon rocket zip along the fishing line and reach the opposite end?   **YES   NO**

   If not, how far did the rocket travel? _____

3. Compare the flight of your rocket to that of other teams. What did you notice?

MAKING BALLOON ROCKETS

ROCKET LAUNCH 2

1. Make any adjustments you need to your team rocket or Rocket Launch Zone. Describe your adjustments. _____

   _____

2. Prepare for a second launch. Each teammate should change roles for the second launch.
3. Launch the rocket a second time.
4. Record the distance traveled. Compute the difference between the two launches.

   LAUNCH 1 _____

   LAUNCH 2 _____

   DIFFERENCE(S) BETWEEN THE TWO LAUNCHES _____

   _____

VARIATIONS

1. Try using a different style or size balloon. Try a large, round balloon, a twisty type, or a super long balloon.
2. Which balloon worked best? _____
3. Why do you think it worked so well? _____

   _____

DISTANCE CONTEST

1. Set up the longest fishing line runway you can make inside or outside. It should be longer than 30 feet.
2. Take turns testing each balloon rocket to see how far and how fast along the line it will travel.
3. Have a partner time each flight and fill in the chart to the right.

ROCKET	SPEED	DISTANCE

4. Whose rocket traveled the fastest? _____
5. Look at the rocket and try to determine why it was the fastest.

   _____

   _____

6. Draw your rocket "in flight" on the back of this page.

MAKING BALLOON ROCKETS

JOURNAL ENTRY

1. What was the longest distance your balloon rocket traveled in a single flight? _____

   _____

2. Which kind of balloon provided the longest ride for your rocket? _____

   _____

   Why do you think this balloon went so far? _____

   _____

   _____

3. What kind of balloon was the least successful at moving your rocket? _____

   _____

   Why? _____

   _____

   _____

4. What was the most difficult part of the launch? _____

   _____

   What did you do to make it work better? _____

   _____

   _____

5. What did you learn today that surprised you? _____

   _____

   _____

DESIGN PROCESS REVIEW—MAKING BALLOON ROCKETS

Share your responses, documents, and experiences and, if possible, demonstrate your balloon rockets with your classmates in a class discussion led by your teacher.

CHALLENGE: DESIGN A TYPE OF AIR TRANSPORTATION

Directions: Design a flying machine of your own. Plan on using materials from past activities in the unit and other teacher-approved materials from the classroom or recycling area.

BRAINSTORM: Think about what you have learned about the movement of air or wind, objects that fly, and the effect of air on moving objects.

Was there a helicopter or rocket you have already made that you would like to do again with an improved design? Would you like to make it bigger, smaller, wider, or heavier? Perhaps there is another design idea you would like to try or a combination of ideas.

What would you like to make for this challenge and why? _____

_____

Where did your ideas come from? _____

_____

Will you need to do extra research?   **YES   NO**

If so, what do you want to find out? _____

_____

DESIGN THE SOLUTION: Sketch your plan in the box below. Label it. Add notes if needed.

```
                                          _____
                                          _____
                                          _____
                                          _____
                                          _____
                                          _____
                                          _____
                                          _____
```

BUILD: Use materials from Activities 1–3 in order to build your new model. Check with your teacher if you wish to add other materials to the design. When finished, take it for a test run!

What materials are you using? _____

_____

_____

Ⓝ Ⓐ Ⓜ Ⓔ _____

CHALLENGE: DESIGN A TYPE OF AIR TRANSPORTATION

EVALUATE: What type of testing did you do? _____

_____

_____

Did your design work as you'd planned?   **YES   NO**

Explain: _____

_____

MODIFY: What adjustments can you make to improve the flight of your vehicle? List them and sketch your modifications in the space below.

_____

_____

_____

_____

_____

_____

_____

_____

_____

_____

SHARE: Describe the results of your project.

_____

_____

_____

Explain what you or any student could learn from this project.

_____

_____

_____

SIMPLE MACHINES

6 sessions: 1 session for each activity (approximately 1 to $1\frac{1}{2}$ hours per session). For this unit, you may wish to divide the class and have different groups work on the different machines and then rotate. It will depend upon the amount of time and materials you can generate. If six groups are formed, they can be broken down further into pairs. At the end of the unit, students can share their findings for each of the simple machines.

Focus: Physical Science, Physics—simple machines

CONNECTIONS AND SUGGESTIONS

SCIENCE—This unit explores the six simple machines—the wheel and axle, the wedge, the inclined plane, the lever, the pulley, and the screw. Students will examine the applications of simple machines in school and life. They will compare three classes of levers. They will be encouraged to spot six simple machines and identify how they are used in day-to-day life.

TECHNOLOGY—Students can use basic computer software or personal tablets to do research on simple machines and to record research notes, ideas, and responses as they build machines. They may also use cameras and/or video equipment to take photographs or film their explorations of simple machines.

ENGINEERING—Students will examine and experiment with each of the six simple machines to see how they work. They will be able to test the machines and see how to reduce the amount of effort needed to do certain tasks. They will observe combinations of simple machines like wheels and axles and levers to see how they combine to make more complex machines (bicycle).

MATH—Students will take accurate measurements of length using appropriate tools. The activities in this unit require the manipulation of a variety of rectangular, cubic, and triangular geometric shapes to create the three types of levers and other simple machines. The measurement applications in this unit require students to make comparisons of weight, surface area, length, and width. Students will measure different solid materials to create new products.

DISCUSSION PROMPT: Let's spend a few minutes brainstorming to create a class list of machines we see or use every day. Discuss the machines on the list.

What do these machines have in common?

Do all machines have moving parts?

Did you think of a machine as a device that has a motor?

We will be examining simple machines that do not have motors. It might surprise you to know that the wedge, the inclined plane, and the screw are considered machines even though they do not have moving parts. The reason—*something is considered a machine if it helps us do work.* Simple machines can be small, like the pulley used to move blinds up and down, or huge, like the pulley on a crane. Many of the machines on our list make use of one or more very simple machines.

SIMPLE MACHINES

UNIT MATERIALS (for a class of 30 to 35)

- ☐ 2 pans or large bowls
- ☐ $3\frac{1}{2}$–4", thin rubber bands
- ☐ 6" or 8", thin rubber bands
- ☐ 6" × 3", stiff cardboard or cardstock
- ☐ 8" × 4", stiff cardboard or cardstock
- ☐ 12"–18" PVC pipe or waterproof tube
- ☐ 36" clear plastic tubing
- ☐ dowels or rods
- ☐ fishing line
- ☐ large tongue depressors
- ☐ masking tape
- ☐ nails (to make holes in plastic cups)
- ☐ newsprint

- ☐ paper clips (large)
- ☐ pencils
- ☐ protractor
- ☐ regular plastic straws
- ☐ rulers (standard and metric)
- ☐ scissors
- ☐ spools (wooden, plastic, or other)
- ☐ spring scale
- ☐ thin, plastic stirrers
- ☐ water bottle caps (at least 4 to a team)
- ☐ wooden barbeque skewers
- ☐ wooden cubes
- ☐ wooden triangular prisms (or blocks)

FIND OUT MORE

Bill Nye the Science Guy S01E10 Simple Machines
https://www.youtube.com/
Check *youtube.com* for a variety of age-appropriate videos about different simple machines presented by Bill Nye.

Discovery Center of Idaho: Science Trek—Simple Machines
Excellent, age-appropriate explanations and examples of 6 simple machines
https://www.youtube.com/watch?v=Kg_vZ2pgQEs

Safety Note: All websites should be checked prior to student viewing to be certain that content is appropriate.

SIMPLE MACHINES VOCABULARY

complex machine—a combination of simple machines

dolly—a piece of equipment with wheels and an axle, used to move heavy items

effort—the amount of energy needed to move or lift an object

force—strength or energy exerted; cause of motion or change; active power

fulcrum—the support for a lever as it lifts an object; the pivot point

inclined plane—a simple machine for lifting and moving; a simple machine that makes it easier to push or pull loads; a ramp

lever—a simple machine used to lift an object. A basic lever is a flat surface (bar) balanced on a fulcrum. The load is placed on one end of the bar and force, or effort, is placed on the other end.

load—the object being moved, lifted, or carried

machine—a device used to move, cut, or do other work. There are simple machines like a lever and complex machines like a bike, which is made up of more than one machine.

Parts of a Lever

force

load

fulcrum

pulley—a simple machine used to lift and move objects. A basic pulley is a wheel with a grooved rim, around which a rope passes. It is used to raise or move objects from one place to another.

screw—a cylinder with an inclined plane wrapped around it. A screw is a simple machine used to join two things together by being rotated.

🚫 Slot head

✖ Phillips head

tool—a device held in one's hand that is used to carry out a function. For example, a screwdriver is a tool used to screw in a screw (a simple machine).

wedge—a simple, V-shaped machine that can be used to separate or divide objects (an ax), lift up an object, or hold an object in place (a doorstop)

wheel and axle—a simple machine used to move things. An axle is a rod that goes through a wheel and allows it to turn.

work—the effort used to move a load

SIMPLE MACHINES

WHO KNEW?

MACHINES

MACHINES

There are six *simple machines*. You can build almost anything with these six machines. They are the building blocks of all other machines.

These simple machines work with our muscles to help us do things. Lifting things is easier when we use machines to help us. Moving things from one place to another place is easier, too.

Simple machines also help us work faster.

Here are the six simple machines:

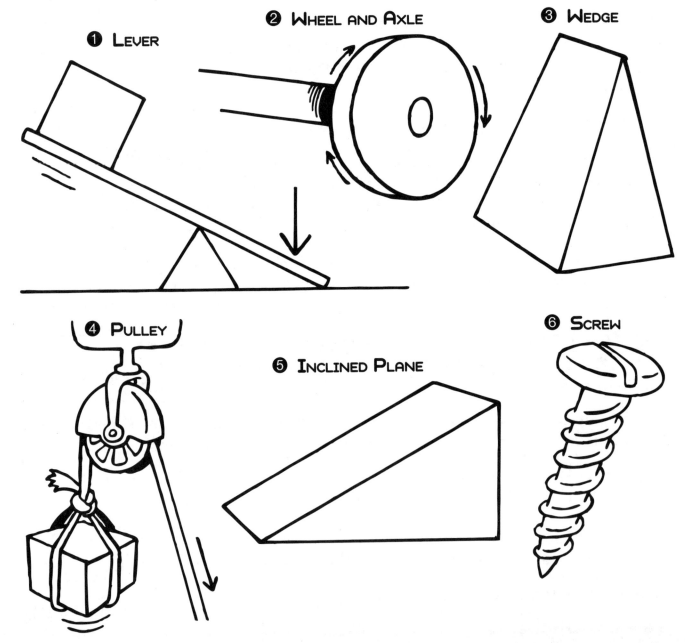

❶ **LEVER**

❷ **WHEEL AND AXLE**

❸ **WEDGE**

❹ **PULLEY**

❺ **INCLINED PLANE**

❻ **SCREW**

SIMPLE MACHINES

Directions: Use with page 114. Look at the pictures of machines we use. Write the number of the simple machine you see from page 114. The first one has been done for you.

MOVING DAY—SIMPLE MACHINES TO THE RESCUE

It is moving day at our house, and we are very excited. We have to move all of our things from our old house to the new house. How will we do that?

First, we removed the **screws** from the front door hinges and took the doors down. That made a bigger opening to get things through. Then, we put **wedges,** called doorstops, under the other doors to keep them from swinging.

The movers will use **inclined planes** called "ramps" to move heavy items. They will use something called a dolly. It has **wheels and an axle** on the bottom to pull heavy items up the ramp. Later, they will use the dolly to move items back out of the truck.

The pictures have been taken down, and now we need to get those nails out of the wall. We can use the handle of a hammer as a **lever.** Then the claw part of the hammer will pull the nails out.

Dad's old car also has to be moved from the driveway. The car doesn't work, but he wants to keep it. Luckily, the tires are still good. Dad called his friend to bring over a tow truck. They will use the **pulley** to lift up the front end of the car and tow the car to the new house!

1. Explain how each simple machine was used to help on moving day.

    INCLINED PLANE—_____

    _____

    LEVER—_____

    _____

    PULLEY—_____

    _____

    SCREW—_____

    _____

    WEDGE—_____

    _____

    WHEEL AND AXLE—_____

    _____

2. Use the *Ways to Use Simple Machines* checklist on page 116 to keep track of the six simple machines you see. Keep adding to it throughout the unit.

THREE TYPES OF LEVERS

A lever is a simple machine that changes the amount of force needed to do a job. If you shovel snow, dig a hole, or swing a baseball bat, you are using a lever. There are three parts to every lever—the lifting bar, the fulcrum, and the load (or effort).

The **lifting bar** is the part used to move an object.

The **fulcrum** is the pivoting point that the lifting bar is leaning against.

The **load** is where the effort (force) takes place to lift or move something.

THREE CLASSES OF LEVERS

There are three classes or types of levers. To tell which is which, look at the fulcrum.

1. In a class 1 lever, the fulcrum is between the load and the force.

FORCE

LOAD

FULCRUM

Examples:  **seesaw**    **crowbar**   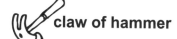 **claw of hammer**

2. In a class 2 lever, the load is between the force and the fulcrum.

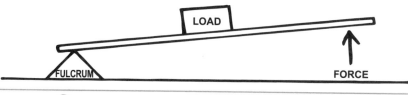

LOAD

FULCRUM

FORCE

Examples:  **wheelbarrow**    **bottle opener**

3. In a class 3 lever, the distance is magnified, and the force is applied between the fulcrum and the load.

LOAD

FULCRUM   FORCE

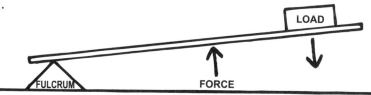

Examples:  **tongs**    **human arm**    **broom**

WAYS TO USE SIMPLE MACHINES

Directions: Here is a list of simple machines. Check off each machine you use or see working. Keep this list handy, and check off other machines as you observe them.

LEVER

Class 1
- [ ] balance scale
- [ ] crowbar
- [ ] scissors
- [ ] seesaw

Class 2
- [ ] bottle opener
- [ ] brake pedal (car)
- [ ] nutcracker
- [ ] wheelbarrow

Class 3
- [ ] broom
- [ ] human jaw
- [ ] tongs
- [ ] tweezers

PULLEY

- [ ] clothesline
- [ ] crane
- [ ] fishing pole

- [ ] flag pole
- [ ] move blinds up and down
- [ ] open and close curtains

- [ ] pull up water from a well

WHEEL AND AXLE

- [ ] bicycle
- [ ] bus

- [ ] car
- [ ] doorknobs

- [ ] knobs on radio, stove, etc.
- [ ] system used to pull maps and blinds up and down

INCLINED PLANE

- [ ] funnel
- [ ] ramp

- [ ] playground slide
- [ ] skateboard ramp

- [ ] wheelchair ramp

WEDGE

- [ ] airplane wing
- [ ] ax

- [ ] chisel
- [ ] knife

- [ ] saw
- [ ] wedge for door

SCREW

- [ ] drill (bit)
- [ ] jar (screw top keeps lid on jar)

- [ ] screw

- [ ] spiral staircase

LEVERS

Directions: Each picture on this page shows one or two levers. Highlight each lever. Then circle the fulcrum for each machine. Remember, a class 2 or class 3 lever has the fulcrum on the end.

CLASS 1	CLASS 2	CLASS 3

WORKING WITH LEVERS

Directions: As a class, review the three types of levers (page 117) before beginning the activity. Then, pair up, gather materials, and begin working with levers.

> ### TEAM MATERIALS
> - 12" standard rulers (wooden or stiff plastic)
> - $3\frac{1}{2}$"–4", thin rubber bands
> - large tongue depressors
> - masking tape
>
> - pencils
> - 30 cm metric rulers (wooden or stiff plastic)
> - wooden cubes or oversized blocks
> - wooden triangular blocks (prisms)

CLASS 1 LEVERS

In a class 1 lever, the fulcrum is between the load and the force. Good examples of class 1 levers are a seesaw and a balance scale.

MAKE A CLASS 1 LEVER—TONGUE DEPRESSOR

1. Assemble a class 1 lever. Use a triangular prism, a tongue depressor, and a cube.
2. Place the prism *(fulcrum)* directly under the center of the tongue depressor.
3. Use a small piece of rolled masking tape on the bottom center of the tongue depressor *(force)* to keep it from sliding around as it pivots on the triangular prism.
4. Does it balance? If not, adjust.

USE A CLASS 1 LEVER—TRIAL 1—TONGUE DEPRESSOR

1. Place the wooden cube *(load)* at the far end of the tongue depressor.
2. Use one finger to press down on the upper, empty end of the tongue depressor.

   What happens? _____
3. Press down again to make the lever even on both sides. Feel the amount of pressure you need to hold the lever even at both ends.

   What was the difference? _____

   _____

MOVE THE FULCRUM—TRIAL 1—TONGUE DEPRESSOR

1. Move the fulcrum away from your finger. It should be $\frac{3}{4}$ of the way down the tongue depressor—away from your finger.
2. Press down again to compare the amount of pressure you need now to hold the lever even at both ends.
3. Describe the difference from the first test. _____

   _____

WORKING WITH LEVERS

OBSERVATION—TRIAL 1—TONGUE DEPRESSOR

1. Does it take more or less force to lift the load (cube) when the fulcrum is nearer to it?

MORE   LESS

Why? _____

What is the difference? _____

USE A CLASS 1 LEVER—TRIAL 2—RULER

1. Do the same lever experiment using a ruler instead of a tongue depressor. Choose a ruler that will not bend.
2. Place the fulcrum under the middle of the ruler.
3. Place a block on one end of the lever.
4. Use one finger to press down on the empty end of the ruler. Feel the amount of pressure you need to hold the lever even at both ends.

5. Describe what happened. _____

_____

_____

MOVE THE FULCRUM—TRIAL 2—RULER

1. Place the ruler on the fulcrum so that the fulcrum is $\frac{3}{4}$ of the way from the force—where you press down on the ruler.
2. Did it take more or less force to lift the load (*cube*) when you moved the fulcrum farther away from it.

MORE   LESS

3. Move the fulcrum closer to the force. Sketch your new lever. Does it take more or less force to lift the load (*cube*) when you moved the fulcrum closer?

MORE   LESS

OBSERVATION—TRIAL 2—RULER

1. Why do you think it took more force with a ruler than with a tongue depressor? _____

_____

_____

_____

WORKING WITH LEVERS

Directions: Use a metric ruler and a thin, $3\frac{1}{2}$–4" rubber band or a spring scale to measure the force of your class 1 lever. Use the lever materials from the previous activity.

MEASURING THE FORCE OF CLASS 1 LEVERS

For more accuracy, use a metric ruler to measure the force. Position the pushing end of the ruler so that it is off the desk. Place one end of the rubber band on the end of the ruler. Use a piece of masking tape to keep the rubber band in place near the end of the ruler. Use the length of the rubber band from the ruler to record the force needed to lift the cube.

TEST 1

1. Position the ruler so that the 6" line is exactly above the triangular prism. Gently pull down on the rubber band to lift the ruler so that the cube at the other end of the ruler is sitting on a level ruler.
2. Use the metric ruler to measure the length of the stretched rubber band.
3. Record the length of the stretched rubber band when the ruler is level. _____ **millimeters**

TEST 2

1. Position the ruler so that the 3" line is exactly above the triangular prism. This is 9" away from the pushing end of the ruler.
2. Gently pull down on the rubber band to lift the ruler so that the cube at the end of the ruler is sitting on a level ruler. (You may need to extend the ruler over the end of the desk.)
3. Use the metric ruler to measure the length of the stretched rubber band.
4. Record the length of the stretched rubber band when the ruler is level. _____ **millimeters**

TEST 3

1. Position the first ruler so that at the 9" line is exactly above the triangular prism. (This is 3" away from the pushing end of the ruler.)
2. Gently pull down on the rubber band to lift the ruler so that the cube at the end of the ruler is sitting on a level ruler.
3. Use the metric ruler to measure the length of the stretched rubber band.
4. Record the length of the stretched rubber band when the ruler is level. _____ **millimeters**

DRAWING CONCLUSIONS

What conclusion can you make about moving the fulcrum if you are using a lever?

_____

_____

WORKING WITH LEVERS

Directions: Assemble a class 2 lever by using a cube (*load*), a ruler (*force*) and a triangular prism (*fulcrum*).

CLASS 2 LEVERS

In a class 2 lever, the load is between the force and the fulcrum. Instead of being in the middle, the fulcrum is on one end. Good examples of class 2 levers are a wheelbarrow and a bottle cap opener. Nail clippers and nutcrackers use *two* class 2 levers.

MAKE A CLASS 2 LEVER

1. Place the end of a ruler above the fulcrum.
2. Lay the second end of the ruler on the table.
3. Position the load on the center of the ruler.
4. Tape the rubber band on the bottom of the ruler that is on the table.
5. Explain how a class 2 lever works.

MEASURING THE FORCE OF A CLASS 2 LEVER

1. Hold the rubber band up and measure its height. _____ **millimeters**.
2. Lift the ruler by using the rubber band until the ends of the ruler are level.
3. Measure the length of the rubber band.
4. How many millimeters did it take to lift the cube? _____ **millimeters**.

MOVE THE LOAD AND MEASURE

Place the load at the 9" mark on the ruler (3" from the fulcrum). How many millimeters did the rubber band stretch in raising the cube?

_____ **millimeters**

Place the cube at the 3" mark on the ruler (9" from the fulcrum). How many millimeters did the rubber band stretch in raising the cube?

_____ **millimeters**

Place the cube at the 1" mark on the ruler (11" from the fulcrum). How many millimeters did the rubber band stretch in raising the cube?

_____ **millimeters**

NAME _____

WORKING WITH LEVERS

CLASS 3 LEVERS

Directions: Assemble a class 3 lever by using tape and two tongue depressors.

Class 3 levers place the effort between the load and the fulcrum. The fulcrum is on one end like a class 2 lever. The load is at the other end, and the effort is moved to the middle. Good examples of third class levers are tongs and tweezers. These two machines each have two class 3 levers. The human arm is also a class-three lever.

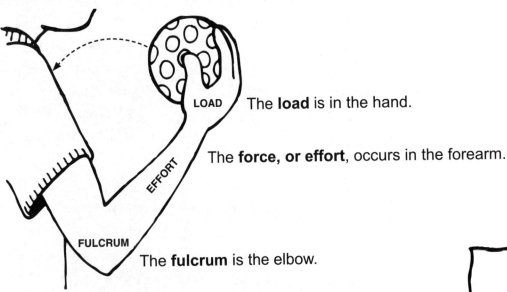

The **load** is in the hand.

The **force, or effort**, occurs in the forearm.

The **fulcrum** is the elbow.

MAKE A CLASS 3 LEVER

1. Create a pair of tweezers or tongs by taping two tongue depressors together at one end in order to form a hinge. This hinge of tape creates the fulcrum.

USE A CLASS 3 LEVER

1. Hold the tongs together near the hinge.

2. Use the open end of the tongue depressors in order to pick up objects such as the cube, an eraser, pencil, or other loads.

3. Explain how a class 3 lever works. _____

   _____

4. What could you do to this lever to make it work better? _____

   _____

   _____

WORKING WITH LEVERS

JOURNAL ENTRY

1. Why do you think that a fulcrum often has a triangular shape? _____

   _____

   What other shape might work? _____

2. List 3 examples of levers that you see every day.

   _____   _____   _____

3. Name a common lever you use. _____

   Which class does it belong to?   (1)   (2)   (3)

   How do you use this lever? _____

   _____

   Draw this lever and label the *load,* the *force,* and the *fulcrum* in the space below.

4. Where are the force, the load, and the fulcrum located on a wheelbarrow? _____

   _____

DESIGN PROCESS REVIEW—WORKING WITH LEVERS

Share your experiences, journal entries, and other documents about building and using levers in a class discussion led by your teacher.

THE WEDGE AND THE INCLINED PLANE

THE WEDGE

The *wedge* is a very simple machine and a very useful tool. Wedges can be used to split wood or to hold things, like a door, in place.

Directions: Work in pairs to make and test wedges.

TEAM MATERIALS

- $3\frac{1}{2}$"–4", thin rubber bands
- cardboard or cardstock
- masking tape
- newsprint
- pencils
- protractors
- rulers
- scissors
- small weighted object
- spring scale (optional)

MAKING WEDGES

1. Use a piece of stiff cardboard. Cut a strip 1" wide and 6" long.
2. Fold the piece over 2" from one end. Make a sharp crease.
3. Fold the strip again $\frac{1}{2}$" from the first fold. Make another sharp crease.
4. Measure 2" farther along the strip and fold again. Tape the cardboard into a triangular shape.
5. Stuff the leftover pieces of cardboard inside of the wedge. Use tape to hold the stuffed wedge together.

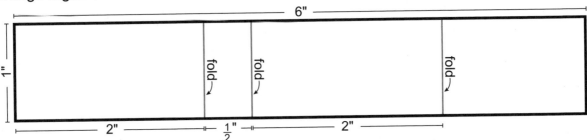

USING WEDGES

Wedges made of metal are used to separate logs. An ax is a type of wedge that has a handle. The metal end of the ax is the wedge. The handle of the ax acts like a lever. The wedge magnifies the power of a force. The blade end of the ax magnifies the force applied. When the ax is swung into a chunk of wood, the wood splits.

1. What are some uses of wedges made of other materials? _____

_____

2. What can you do with the cardboard wedge you made? Think about separating books, stacks of paper, and other materials in your desk and in the classroom. List some classroom uses for your paper wedge. Be creative.

_____   _____   _____

3. Try out your ideas for a cardboard wedge. Circle the uses that worked.
4. List two uses for heavier, metal or rubber wedges. Circle any you have actually used.

_____   _____

THE WEDGE AND THE INCLINED PLANE

Directions: Work in pairs to make and compare inclined planes. See if they do make lifting heavy objects easier. You will need cardboard, rubber bands, a small weighted object, newsprint, and tape.

WORKING WITH AN INCLINED PLANE

The word *incline* means "at an angle." An inclined plane resembles a wedge, but it is used in a different way. One use of an inclined plane is something you may see every day—a ramp. Ramps are often used to move heavy items onto and off of trucks. A metal dolly can also be used on the inclined plane to move items up or down the inclined plane.

A flight of stairs is another example of an inclined plane—think of the angle of the stairs. Isn't it easier to walk up the stairs than it would be to climb to the next level?

The slides you see in the park are inclined planes too!

MAKING THE INCLINED PLANE

1. Cut one strip of heavy cardboard about 8" × 4".
2. Measure 2" down the length of the strip. Draw a line across the width of the material at the 2" mark.
3. Use a stiff ruler or the edge of the desk in order to fold or bend the cardboard.
4. Tape the cardboard at a 60-degree angle. Stuff under it with newsprint if you need added support.

Using the Inclined Plane

1. Wrap two thin rubber bands around the small, heavy object. Tape the rubber bands in an "X" shape at the bottom of the item and leave the other ends loose at the top. You will hold the item by the loose ends of the rubber bands.

2. Place the item with the rubber bands next to the top of the inclined plane. Loop the loose ends of the rubber bands around your finger. Use the bands to carefully lift the item to the height of the top of the ramp. Notice how heavy it feels.

3. Use a ruler to measure the length of the rubber bands from the top of the item to your finger. Use the centimeter/millimeter scale and record the number below. If you have a spring scale, take a second measurement.

   Number of millimeters (ruler): _____ **Number of millimeters (spring scale):** _____

4. Next, place the same item and rubber band arrangement on the bottom of the ramp. Loop the rubber band and gently pull the block up the ramp.

5. Use a ruler to measure the length of the rubber bands from the top of the block to your finger. Use the centimeter/millimeter scale again and record the number below. Do the same with a spring scale if one is available.

   Number of millimeters (ruler): _____ **Number of millimeters (spring scale):** _____

THE WEDGE AND THE INCLINED PLANE

JOURNAL ENTRY

1. How are the wedge and the inclined plane the same? _____

   _____

   _____

2. How are the wedge and the inclined plane different? _____

   _____

   _____

3. If you had to move a cement block up a flight of stairs, which simple machine would you use?

   WEDGE   **INCLINED PLANE**

   Explain your answer. _____

   _____

   _____

4. Which simple machine would be most useful to a man splitting logs?

   WEDGE   **INCLINED PLANE**

   Explain your answer. _____

   _____

   _____

5. How does the stretched rubber band show the amount of effort needed to lift or move the block with or without an inclined plane?

   _____

   _____

   _____

DESIGN PROCESS REVIEW—THE WEDGE AND THE INCLINED PLANE

Share your experiences, journal entries, and other documents about building and using wedges and inclined planes in a class discussion led by your teacher.

THE WHEEL AND AXLE

The *wheel and axle* is probably the most common simple machine in the world. Wheels turn on an axle. You can see examples of wheels everywhere. Wheels open doors (door knobs) and help turn stoves on. Wheels are found on cars, wagons, bikes, and buses.

Wheels help move people and things. The invention of the wheel and axle changed the way people work. The wheel and axle made it possible to move a heavy load without having to carry it.

It also changed the way people travel. People could go to more places and get there faster. They could travel in wagons or later on bikes, cars, trains, or buses.

Directions: Work in teams of two to make two wagons. Take turns doing the pulling and the measuring.

TEAM MATERIALS
- 6" or 8" thin rubber bands
- cube or weighted object
- masking tape
- plastic straws (regular and coffee stirrers)
- rulers
- scissors
- stiff cardboard
- thin nail or other pointed object (math compass)
- thin water bottle caps (at least 4 per team)
- wooden barbeque skewers

MAKING A SMALL WAGON

1. Cut or trim a piece of stiff cardboard about 6" × 3".

2. Cut two 3" pieces from a plastic straw.

3. Arrange one 3" straw on the short end of cardboard, 1" from the end. Make sure the straw is straight and even from the end of the cardboard. Use masking tape to hold it in place.

4. Arrange the other 3" piece of the straw 1" from the other end of the cardboard. Use masking tape to hold it in place. It should be even from the end of the cardboard.

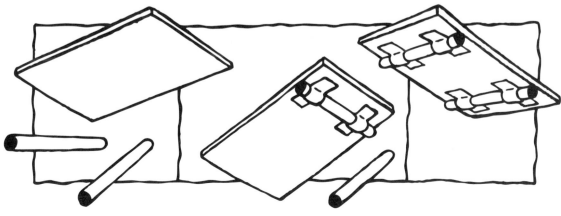

N A M E

THE WHEEL AND AXLE

MOUNTING THE WHEELS

1. With adult help, use the point of a thin nail or math compass to make a small hole in the center of four thin, plastic water-bottle caps.

2. Wiggle the sharp item around once the hole is made in order to make the opening large enough to fit the stirrer.

3. Carefully insert the thin plastic stirrer into one bottle cap about 1". The opening of the cap should be facing out. The plastic stirrer is the axle.

4. Slide this stirrer axle through the larger straw already attached to the cardboard.

5. Place the other end of the stirrer axle through a second water-bottle cap.

6. Make your second axle the same way as described above.

TESTING YOUR SMALL WAGON

1. Place your cube or weighted object that has the taped-on rubber bands on one side of the desk. Take the rubber bands and pull the object across the desk. Stop and measure the length of the thin rubber bands from your fingers to the cube as the rubber bands drag the cube across the desk. Record the length below.

   Length of the rubber bands dragging the cube: _____ **mm**

2. Place the cube on the small wagon you just made. Pull it across the desk again by the rubber bands. Stop and measure the length of the thin rubber bands from your fingers to the cube as the rubber bands drag the cube on the wagon across the desk. Record the length below.

   Length of the rubber bands dragging the wagon and cube: _____ **mm**

BUILD A BIGGER WAGON

Directions: Create a stronger or faster-moving wagon in order to transport more wooden blocks or other weights. Use more wheels, a larger base, a stronger axle, or a new design.

KEEP THE FOLLOWING GUIDELINES IN MIND:

—The base must be no larger than 8" × 3". It must be made of cardboard or heavy paper.

—You may not use more than 5 straws and 5 stirrers or wooden skewers.

—Up to 10 water-bottle caps can be used.

1. Sketch your plan in the frame.

2. Build your bigger wagon.

3. Test the bigger wagon.

★ ★ ★ SAVE YOUR WAGONS ★ ★ ★

THE WHEEL AND AXLE

JOURNAL ENTRY

1. What part of the wagon made it easier to move? _____

    _____

    _____

2. How well would a wagon work without wheels? _____

    Explain. _____

    _____

    _____

3. Did larger wheels move the block more easily than the smaller wheels?   **YES   NO**

    Explain your answer. _____

    _____

    _____

4. What other materials could you use for wheels?

    _____   _____   _____

5. What was the most interesting information you learned doing this activity? _____

    _____

    _____

6. Write down four uses for the wheel and axle that you see or use. Put a check in the box
    next to the one you think is the most important.

    ☐ _____

    ☐ _____

    ☐ _____

    ☐ _____

DESIGN PROCESS REVIEW—THE WHEEL AND THE AXLE

Share your responses, documents, and experiences with your classmates in a class
discussion led by your teacher. Demonstrate your small wagons if time allows.

THE SCREW

The *screw* is a simple machine. It is an inclined plane wrapped around a pole. Most of us think of a screw as something you screw into wood with a screwdriver. That is the most common example. Another one is a jar with a lid. Look at the top where you twist on the lid. That is a screw, too!

One of the most famous uses of this simple machine is *Archimedes' Screw*. Archimedes was a great scientist and inventor. He designed this large screw to help bring water from a river to water crops. The water was down the hill from the crops.

Directions: Work in pairs to create a system that moves water from a low level to a higher level. Create a model similar to Archimedes' Screw.

TEAM MATERIALS
- 2 pans or large bowls (need to hold at least 3" of water)
- 12"–18" PVC pipe or waterproof tube
- 36" clear plastic tubing
- masking tape or duct tape
- *optional:* food coloring

MAKE A MODEL OF ARCHIMEDES' SCREW

1. Tape one end of the plastic tubing to one end of the PVC pipe.	2. Wrap the plastic tubing around the pipe to create a spiral, like a screw. The tubing has to be at an incline and must go up the pipe.

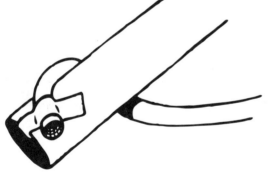

3. Tape the tubing at the other end of the PVC pipe.	4. Make sure the tubing is secure on both sides.

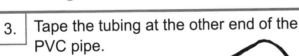

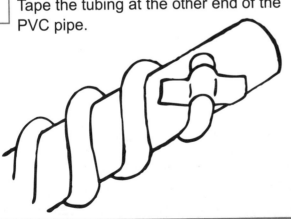

THE SCREW

TEST THE MODEL OF ARCHIMEDES' SCREW

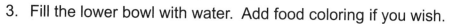

1. Set up the two pans or bowls. One should be on the table and the other one should be on a stack of blocks, or a box. Use something that can get wet and not a stack of books!

2. Place one end of your machine in the bowl on the table and rest the other one on the edge of the top bowl. Hold the device at about a 30-degree angle.

3. Fill the lower bowl with water. Add food coloring if you wish.

4. Turn your "screw" and watch as the water rises on the coiled tubing.

   Describe what is happening. _____

   _____

   Is it working?   **YES**   **NO**

5. Sketch your setup in the frame below and show the water moving up.

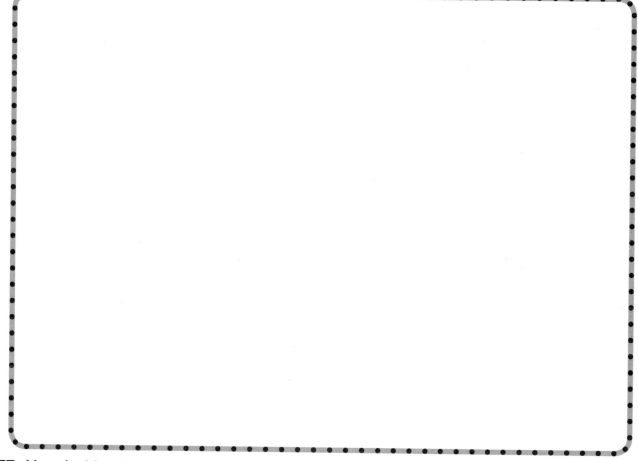

NOTE: Your Archimedes' Screw should create a flow of water along the curved tube from the pan at the bottom to the pan at the top.

THE PULLEY

Directions: Work in pairs or small groups to make pulleys. Compare them and determine if they can make it easier to lift heavy objects.

TEAM MATERIALS

- fishing line
- large paper clips and/or modeling clay
- masking tape
- rulers
- spools

- stacks of books
- thin rod or dowel
- thin rubber bands
- wooden or plastic spools, or other round object with elevated edges

NOTE: The dowel or rod will need to fit through the hole in the spool. Wooden spools can be found at craft stores. Often, fabric stores have plastic spools from ribbon. Other sources can be found online.

THE PULLEY

The pulley is a simple machine that uses a wheel and axle and rope or string. A pulley changes the direction of force when lifting or moving an object. You pull down to lift something up!

MAKE A PULLEY

1. Make two equal stacks of books about 8" high. Place them on a table about 8"–10" apart.
2. Slide the spool onto the rod.
3. Tape the rod on top of the two stacks of books, connecting them like a bridge. Move the spool to the center of the two stacks.
4. Tape 6 large paper clips together to form a bob (weight). Each paper clip weighs about 2 grams (depending on the maker), so the weight of this bob is about 12 grams.
5. Cut a 16" piece of fishing line and tie one end to the end of the paper clip bob.

TEST THE PULLEY

1. Hold the other end of the line with your thumb and forefinger over the spool. The paper clip bob should rest on the table beneath the spool.
2. Pull the line you are holding down over the spool to lift the paper clip bob that is on the other side.
3. Do this several times to see how the pulley functions. What do you notice? _____

_____

ADD A SECOND PULLEY WHEEL

1. Place a second rod that has another round spool about 4"–5" up the stack of books. Center the second spool directly below the first spool.
2. Find a way to wrap the fishing line around both pulleys to move the bob.
3. Do several trials. Test this pulley arrangement as you did the other one.
4. Does the second pulley make it easier to lift the bob?   **YES   NO**

Explain. _____

THE PULLEY

JOURNAL ENTRY

1. Where have you seen pulleys in use? _____

   _____

2. A pulley changes the direction of force. Explain what that means.

   _____

   _____

   _____

3. What could you use pulleys to do? _____

   _____

4. Do you think using three or four pulleys at a time would make it easier to lift things?

   _____

   Explain. _____

   _____

5. Draw a pulley system you could make that could lift a large rock.

 NAME _____

CHALLENGE: BUILD A MACHINE

You have explored the six simple machines and observed them in your school and at home. Now it is your turn to build a machine. It can be an improvement on a simple machine or you can combine simple machines to create something new. Perhaps you would like to build an inclined plane racetrack to test the speed of the wagons you made, or of small cars.

Directions: Work in pairs or small groups. Plan on using materials from past activities in the unit and other, teacher-approved materials from the classroom or recycling area.

BRAINSTORM: Review the *Ways to Use Simple Machines* checklist. How many of the simple machines listed did you find? _____

Think about what you learned about the six simple machines. Is there a machine you want to build again and improve?   **YES   NO**   _____

Would you like to combine more than one machine to create something new?   **YES   NO**

What would you like to make for this challenge? _____

Explain your choice. _____

_____

Will you need to do extra research?   **YES   NO**

If so, what do you need to find out? _____

_____

DESIGN THE SOLUTION: Sketch your plan here. Label it. Add notes if needed.

BUILD: Use materials from Activities 1–5 in order to build your machine. Check with your teacher if you wish to add other materials to the design. When finished, test it.

What materials are you using? _____

_____

 **NAME** _____

CHALLENGE: BUILD A MACHINE

EVALUATE: What was the most interesting part of the building process? _____

_____

Did your machine work as planned?   **YES**   **NO**

Explain: _____

_____

MODIFY: What adjustments can you make to improve your machine? List them and sketch your modification in the frame below.

ADJUSTMENTS: _____

_____

_____

SHARE: Describe the results of your project. _____

_____

_____

Explain what you or any student could learn from this project. _____

_____

_____

 **6**

CLASSROOM CHEMISTRY

4 sessions: 1 session for each activity (approximately 1 to $1\frac{1}{2}$ hours per session)

Focus: Physical Science—chemistry

CONNECTIONS AND SUGGESTIONS

SCIENCE—Students will be implementing the Scientific Method in order to experiment with simple chemicals, write hidden messages, and study capillary action. They will create invisible fluids and make them reappear. They will learn that the "inks" have a lower temperature at which they oxidize (burn) than paper does. A heat source, such as an iron or a light bulb, will cause the "inks" to oxidize (burn) before the paper burns so the message shows up clearly.

Students will make and handle a solid fluid nicknamed "glop." It is called a non-Newtonian substance because its viscosity is affected by *handling* instead of temperature. Finally, students will explore capillary action.

TECHNOLOGY—Students can use basic computer software or personal tablets to record their observations and responses. They may also use cameras and/or video equipment to take photographs or film their explorations.

ENGINEERING—Students will need to measure the effects of different actions and materials and to judge how each action and material affects the final product.

MATH—Students will be working with units of liquid and solid measures in order to perform experiments. The measurement applications require that students be specific about the amounts of materials used to create new substances, measure strands of color, and mix or separate chemicals.

DISCUSSION PROMPT: Chemistry is the study of the ways materials interact, combine, and change. Most of us have studied water and how it is affected by temperature. We know that water can change from a liquid to a solid if the temperature gets very cold. If the temperature gets boiling hot, water will change again—to steam, which is a gas.

The states of some materials are not affected by temperature but change if they are handled, or touched. These materials are called *non-Newtonian* substances. If you have ever played with Oobleck or Flubber, you have played with a non-Newtonian substance. If you squeeze them very tightly they are hard, but if you let go, they "melt" in your hands. These substances behave like solids and liquids at the same time. They got their name from Isaac Newton, the brilliant British scientist of the 1600s and early 1700s. It was he who discovered that most liquids flowed more easily and had a lower viscosity when exposed to warmer temperatures.

Teacher Note: While talking, prepare and manipulate a bit of Oobleck. (Remember the Dr. Seuss book, *Bartholomew and the Oobleck?*) Simply mix 1 cup water with $1\frac{1}{2}$–2 cups cornstarch. Students will be mesmerized!

Safety Alert: Do remember to toss the Oobleck in the trash when finished. It should never go down a drain.

 **6**

CLASSROOM CHEMISTRY

UNIT MATERIALS (for a class of 30 to 35)

- ☐ 2 oz., 6 oz., 8 oz., and 10 oz. clear plastic cups
- ☐ apple juice
- ☐ baking soda
- ☐ borax
- ☐ celery or carnations
- ☐ clear tape
- ☐ colored pencils
- ☐ cornstarch
- ☐ cotton swabs
- ☐ eye droppers
- ☐ food coloring—variety of colors
- ☐ iron (for clothes)
- ☐ knife (with adult supervision)
- ☐ lamp with exposed bulb
- ☐ lemon juice
- ☐ magnifying glasses
- ☐ measuring cups

- ☐ milk
- ☐ orange juice
- ☐ plain newsprint
- ☐ plastic teaspoons
- ☐ resealable sandwich bags
- ☐ rulers
- ☐ scissors
- ☐ stirrers
- ☐ thin brown packing paper
- ☐ timers, clock, or stopwatches
- ☐ tongs
- ☐ vinegar
- ☐ water—warm and room temperature
- ☐ water-based (washable) markers
- ☐ white facial tissues
- ☐ white glue
- ☐ white paper towels

FIND OUT MORE

Oobleck: The Dr. Seuss Experiment *http://www.instructables.com/id/Oobleck/*

The Scientific Method *https://www.youtube.com/watch?v=T8427L0Wry0* or *https://www.youtube.com/watch?v=bUa-ilQqEv0*

Capillary Action in Plants *https://www.youtube.com/watch?v=w_tc8tlEoBs*

Colored Flowers
https://www.youtube.com/watch?V=y9hprlmck44

Paper Towel Bridge
https://www.youtube.com/watch?v=FAdmTzD46Kg

Safety Note: All websites should be checked prior to student viewing to be certain that content is appropriate.

CLASSROOM CHEMISTRY VOCABULARY

capillary action—the movement of water or watery fluids up very tiny tubes called capillaries

chemistry—the branch of science that identifies the substances that compose matter; the study of the ways materials interact, combine, and change; elements and compounds

compounds—chemical combinations of two or more elements

diffusion—the spreading out of molecules within a solution; scattering

dissolve—to break up, as in a solid breaking up when placed into a liquid. When something dissolves, it seems to disappear.

hypothesis—a serious scientific guess or idea

invisible—something which cannot be seen

Capillary Action

molecule—the smallest particle of an element or compound that retains the properties of the substance

Newtonian substance—a substance that flows more easily and smoothly when it is warm or hot (ex. water, air, motor oil)

non-Newtonian substance—a substance whose ability to flow is affected by a force other than temperature. Touching or handling might be one such force. (Examples: "Oobleck," "Gak," and "Flubber")

reaction—a chemical change; a response

solution—a substance formed by the even mixture of two or more materials within a liquid

texture—feel, appearance, or consistency

viscous—having a thick, sticky consistency between a solid and a liquid (ex. honey, syrup, or lava)

CLASSROOM CHEMISTRY

MAGIC INK

WHO KNEW?

MAGIC INK

Last night, the phone rang and I answered it. It was for my dad, but he was helping my sister with her homework. I said I would take a message. My uncle said it was important that I write down a phone number. I said I would be careful.

I couldn't find a pen, but there was a glass of juice on the table. I dipped my finger in the juice and wrote the numbers very carefully on the paper. Then I went to tell my dad. When we went back to look at the note, it was blank! I told my dad I had written them with juice and he laughed.

I thought he would be mad, but he said he could get the message back. How, I wondered? He got out the iron and started to iron the paper. I had no idea what he was doing. It seemed crazy!

After a few minutes, the numbers started to show. They were brown, but I could read them. Lucky me!

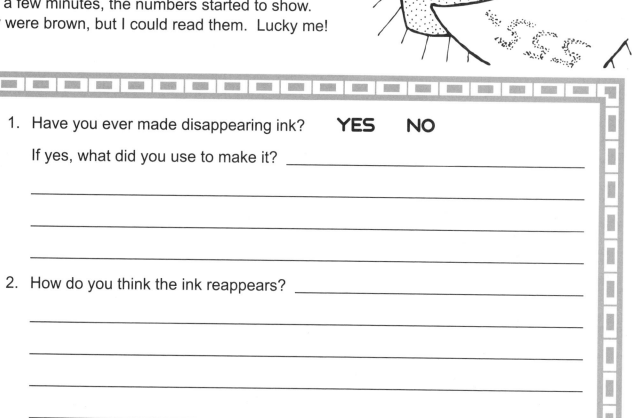

1. Have you ever made disappearing ink?   **YES**   **NO**

   If yes, what did you use to make it? _____

   _____

   _____

   _____

2. How do you think the ink reappears? _____

   _____

   _____

   _____

   _____

TURNING FLOWERS RED

My mom was frustrated. She needed red flowers for a party the following night, and there were none in the garden. She went to the store and they were all out, too. What was she going to do? All of a sudden I heard banging in the kitchen. Then, I heard her say, "Aha!"

When I went to see what was going on, she was holding a small bottle of red food coloring. "I will turn these white flowers red. I will use this food coloring, and they will be ready tomorrow." She cut the stems of the white flowers and put them in the vase of bright red water she had made.

I wondered how that would turn the flowers red since the flower petals weren't in water—just the stems. She just said, "Wait and see!" I was so surprised the next morning when I looked at the vase of flowers. They had turned red, just like mom said they would.

After her party, she explained how it worked. She said the flowers "drank" the red water through their stems. She said the stems acted like straws and brought the water up to the petals to turn them red. She called it **capillary action**. I tried it myself, and I made two blue flowers.

TEST IT

Can you make a carnation or stalk of celery change colors? Try this experiment in the classroom to see the capillary action of a plant at work. You will need the following items:

- knife (ask adult for help cutting)
- measuring cup
- red or blue food coloring
- tall, clear container
- water
- white carnations or celery stalks with tops

1. Fill the clear container with $\frac{1}{2}$ cup water. Add food coloring to create a vibrant color.

2. Ask an adult to help cut the stems or stalks on the diagonal. **Hint:** Use a knife, not scissors—you don't want to crush the ends of the stems! Place the stems or the stalks in the colored water and wait overnight.

3. Did something happen overnight?   **YES   NO**

   If nothing happened, wait a few more days and observe again.

4. Describe what happened to the flower or the celery. _____

   _____

   _____

5. Sketch the capillary action you observed in the box on the right.

NOTE: If you used celery, you may be able to observe the capillary action even more closely. After a few days, break the stalk and peel back the outer layer. You should be able to see the lines of color, like straws, going from one end to the other.

SECRET MESSAGES

Have you ever used disappearing ink? In this activity you and your partner will write three messages using three different liquids. The messages will disappear and then reappear when heat is added.

TEAM MATERIALS

- 2 oz. cups (or large caps)
- 5-minute timer, clock, or stopwatch
- apple juice or orange juice
- cotton swabs
- iron (for the teacher only)
- lemon juice
- light bulb (turned on)
- measuring cups
- milk
- thin brown packing paper
- tongs
- white paper
- white vinegar

⚠ CAUTIONS

☐ ALWAYS keep hands away from face and eyes when handling chemical compounds.

☐ ALWAYS wash your hands when done.

☐ NEVER drink or taste liquids or other substances used in science class.

☐ NEVER touch a hot light bulb (or one that's lit).

☐ NEVER touch a heat source like an iron when it is turned on without adult supervision.

TEACHER PREPARATION

1. Arrange a flat surface where students can place their "coded" messages to dry.

2. Arrange a second area where an iron and a lamp with an exposed bulb can be plugged in. **Safety Alert:** This area will need to be monitored by an adult at all times.

3. Have a serious discussion with your students about the cautions listed above. Explain that they will be approaching their experiments with the same caution a scientist working in a lab would use. Also, discuss the heat factors in these experiments. State clearly that students are not to touch the hot items AND that they are not to do these experiments at home without adult supervision and/or assistance.

4. Duplicate the CAUTION signs below to place near the hot items.

SECRET MESSAGES

Directions: Prepare the first two secret messages as directed. Wait for them to dry (disappear) and then, with adult help, heat them to make them reappear. Use the *Secret Messages* recording sheet on page 147 to record your observations.

SECRET MESSAGE 1

1. Pour 1 ounce of lemon juice into a small cup.

2. Place a cotton swab in the juice to soak for a moment.

3. Use the swab to write a message on plain white paper. Keep dipping the swab in the lemon juice as you write. You may have to do this for every three or four letters.

4. Write one or two sentences on the paper. Use a pen to write the same message here:

_____

_____

5. Use a pen to write your name and the code letter **L** in the upper left corner of the secret message.

6. Let the paper dry for about five minutes while you prepare your next message and materials.

7. Can you see the message you wrote when the paper dries?   **YES   NO**

8. Record your observations for the lemon juice (Message 1) on page 147.

SECRET MESSAGE 2

1. Pour 1 ounce of milk into a small cup.

2. Use a new cotton swab for this message. Let the cotton swab soak in the milk for a moment.

3. Use the swab to write a message on plain white paper. Keep dipping the swab in the milk every few letters.

4. Write one or two sentences on the paper. Use a pen to write the same message here:

_____

_____

5. Use a pen to write your name and the code letter **M** in the upper left corner of the secret message.

6. Let the paper dry for about five minutes while you prepare your next message and materials.

7. Can you see the message you wrote when the paper dries?   **YES   NO**

8. Record your observations for the milk (Message 2) onto page 147.

SECRET MESSAGES

HEATING THE MESSAGES

 CAUTION When the papers with the secret messages are dry, an adult will assist you in applying heat, either by ironing the brown paper over the message, or by holding the white paper next to, but not on, a light bulb. The message should show through.

Directions: Since you are working in pairs, you will be able to compare two different heat methods. For each message, one partner should try the ironing method, and one should try the light bulb method. You can switch methods for each message.

 To prepare for the ironing method, do the following:

1. Place your message inside a folded piece of thin, brown packing paper.
2. Check that the iron is on a medium or medium-high setting.
3. Once the message has been heated, give it to your partner.
4. Can your partner read the secret message you wrote?   **YES**   **NO**

To prepare for the exposed light bulb method, you do not need to use the brown paper.

1. Use tongs to hold the message on the white paper near the bulb.
2. Once the message has been heated, give it to your partner.
3. Can your partner read the secret message you wrote?   **YES**   **NO**

SECRET MESSAGE 3

1. Pour 1 ounce of vinegar into a small cup.
2. Use a new cotton swab for this message. Let the cotton swab soak in the vinegar for a moment.
3. Use the swab to write a message on plain white paper. Keep dipping the swab in the vinegar every few letters.
4. Write one or two sentences on the paper. Use a pen to write the same message here:

_____

_____

5. Use a pen to write your name and the code letter **V** in the upper left corner of the secret message.
6. Let the paper dry for about 5 minutes.
7. Can you see the message you wrote with vinegar when the paper dries?   **YES**   **NO**
8. When the paper of your third message is dry, heat the paper using the iron or a bulb.
9. Can your partner read the secret message you wrote?   **YES**   **NO**
10. Record your observations for the vinegar (Message 3) on page 147.

SECRET MESSAGES

SECRET MESSAGES 4 AND 5

Directions: Work with your partner to test two more "inks" for your secret messages. One partner should use orange juice, and the other partner should use apple juice. Do not dilute the juices.

1. Pour one ounce of apple or one ounce of orange juice into a small cup.

2. Use a new cotton swab for this message. Let the cotton swab soak in the juice for a moment.

3. Use the swab to write a message on plain white paper. Keep dipping the swab in the juice every few letters.

4. Write one or two sentences on the paper. Use a pen to write the same message here:

_____

_____

5. Use a pen to write your name in the upper left corner of the secret message paper. Add either the code letter **A** for apple juice or **O** for orange juice.

6. Let the paper dry for about 5 minutes.

7. Can you see the message you wrote with the juice when the paper dries?   **YES   NO**

8. When the paper of your message is dry, heat the paper using the iron or a bulb.

9. Can your partner read the secret message you wrote?   **YES   NO**

10. Record your observations for the apple juice (Message 4) and the orange juice (Message 5) on page 147. Don't forget to list the type of heat used for each juice.

 NAME _____

SECRET MESSAGES

COMPARE AND CONTRAST

Directions: Use the chart below to record your observations.

SECRET MESSAGES	TYPE OF "INK"	TYPE OF HEAT	RESULTS
MESSAGE 1			☐ CLEAR ☐ UNCLEAR
MESSAGE 2			☐ CLEAR ☐ UNCLEAR
MESSAGE 3			☐ CLEAR ☐ UNCLEAR
MESSAGE 4			☐ CLEAR ☐ UNCLEAR
MESSAGE 5			☐ CLEAR ☐ UNCLEAR

Directions: Study the results of your five secret messages.

1. Which material gave the clearest message?

   LEMON JUICE   MILK   VINEGAR   APPLE JUICE   ORANGE JUICE

2. Do you think this is a good way to send messages?   **YES   NO**

   Explain. _____

   _____

3. Describe the most interesting part of this activity. _____

   _____

   _____

   _____

SECRET MESSAGES

JOURNAL ENTRY

1. Which of your invisible inks was the easiest to read? _____

   Why? _____

   _____

2. Which invisible ink was the most invisible until heated? _____

   _____

3. Which invisible ink did not work or didn't work as well as the others? _____

   _____

   _____

   What might have been the problem? _____

   _____

   _____

4. What element had to be involved to decode all secret writing? _____

   _____

   Why? _____

   _____

5. What is another source of heat that might work? _____

   Why? _____

   _____

6. How might you use the information you learned today in the future? _____

   _____

   _____

SCIENTIFIC METHOD REVIEW—SECRET MESSAGES

Share your journal entries, documents, and experiences with different invisible writing techniques with your classmates during a class discussion led by your teacher.

WORKING WITH GLOP

Directions: Work in pairs as you perform these activities. Read all the directions before beginning.

TEAM MATERIALS

- 6 oz., 8 oz., and 10 oz. clear plastic cups (2 per team)
- borax
- measuring cup
- resealable sandwich bags
- stirrers
- plastic teaspoons
- warm water
- white glue

CAUTIONS

☐ ALWAYS keep hands away from face and eyes when handling chemical compounds.

☐ ALWAYS wash your hands when done.

☐ NEVER drink or taste materials used in science class.

GETTING STARTED—PREPARE THE MIXTURES

CUP 1

1. Pour 2 ounces of glue into the 8 oz. cup.
2. Add 2 ounces of warm water to the 8 oz. cup.
3. Stir the water and glue together until they are completely mixed.

CUP 2

1. Add 2 ounces of warm water to the larger, 10 oz. cup.
2. Add 1 full, rounded teaspoon of borax to the large cup where you just added the warm water.
3. Mix the borax into the water. Use the teaspoon to crunch and smooth out any lumps of borax in the water.
4. Stir the solution until the borax is fully dissolved in the water. The solution should be liquid—but a little thick.

COMBINING CHEMICALS

1. One partner should carefully pour all of the watery glue into the borax solution. At the same time, the other partner should stir the borax solution slowly.
2. Take turns stirring until the material forms into a rubbery, gloppy, gluey mass.
3. Be patient. It will take a few minutes for the liquid to be absorbed.

WORKING WITH GLOP

1. Use your hands to manipulate the material. Together, you and your partner need to pull out this strange substance.

2. Handle the material. Include all the watery, gluey, leftovers that you can.

3. How does this glop react to handling? _____

    _____

    Describe the feel of the material and its reactions. _____

    _____

4. Squeeze out any extra water.

STRETCHING THE GLOP

1. Try stretching the gloppy material. Is it easy to stretch?   **YES   NO**

2. Try wetting the leftover material.

3. Does the glop get harder to stretch or easier to work with?   **HARDER   EASIER**

MAKING SHAPES

1. Squeeze the glop into round shapes—like balls. Try bouncing the glop on a desk or the floor. How does the material react?

    _____

2. Try making a cube shape. Will it form corners?   **YES   NO**

3. Can you make a rectangular object?   **YES   NO**

4. Does the glop keep the shapes you help it form?   **YES   NO**

OTHER MANIPULATIONS

1. Can you make a long, thin "string" like a TV cord?   **YES   NO**

    If yes, how? _____

    _____

2. Can you write on the glop with a pen or marker?   **YES   NO**

3. Make the glop into a flat shape, spread out like a pancake.

    —Can you cut it with a plastic knife?   **YES   NO**

    —Can you tear it easily?   **YES   NO**

SAVING THE GLOP

1. Wet your glop again by dunking it back into the watery cup.

2. Store your glop in a resealable plastic bag. Leave the glop alone until the next science period.

3. Wipe up all the remaining glop and put it in the trash before you wash your hands so the glop does not clog the sink.

★ ★ ★ SAVE THE GLOP ★ ★ ★

WORKING WITH GLOP

JOURNAL ENTRY

1. Have you ever handled a substance like glop before?   **YES**   **NO**

    If yes, what was the substance? _____

    Did it feel the same or did it have a different texture? _____

    _____

    Did it behave the same way? _____

    _____

2. How would you use **glop** to solve a problem? _____

    _____

    _____

    _____

3. What do you think would happen to glop if it was frozen? _____

    _____

    _____

4. How could you make glop a liquid again? _____

    _____

    _____

5. Do you think glop will react differently if you use more glue or more Borax?   **YES**   **NO**

    Explain your answer. _____

    _____

    _____

    _____

SCIENTIFIC METHOD REVIEW—WORKING WITH GLOP

Share your journal entries, documents, and experiences handling glop with your classmates during a class discussion led by your teacher.

NAME _____

CAPILLARY ACTION

Capillary action is one way that liquids are able to move through solids. Plants use capillary action to move water from the soil, through their roots, and up into their stems and leaves.

Today you will use capillary action and water to separate colors in colored marker lines.

Directions: Work in pairs as you perform these activities using markers, water, and soft papers.

TEAM MATERIALS

- 6 oz. or 8 oz. clear plastic cups
- clear tape
- colored pencils
- plain newsprint
- rulers
- scissors
- timer, stopwatch, or clock
- water
- water-soluble markers—red, green, orange, and brown
- white facial tissues

TRIAL 1—PREPARE THE STRIPS AND CUPS

1. Cut five 1" × 6" strips of newsprint.

2. Pull five white facial tissues. Fold each tissue along the middle fold and then fold it in half again so that the tissue strip is about 7" × 1".

3. Pour a little more than an inch of water into the bottom of the clear plastic cup.

4. Use a brightly colored marker to make a wide line at the 3" mark on the newsprint strip. Do not use black or brown.

   What color marker did you use? _____

5. Use the same marker to make a wide line at the mark on a folded, white facial tissue strip.

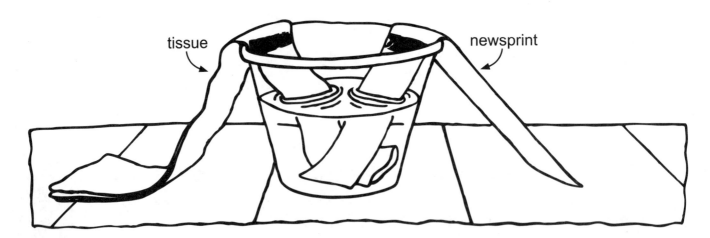

tissue   newsprint

CAPILLARY ACTION

TRIAL 1—OBSERVE THE COLORS

1. Stand the colored end of each strip of soft paper in the water cup. The wide color lines should be above the water, near the middle of the cups.

2. Bend the top of the newsprint and tissue over the lip of the cup. You don't want the strips to slide into the water. If necessary, use clear tape to hold them in place.

3. Record the start time: _____ Plan to watch the reaction for at least 10 minutes.

4. Leave the cup and papers on the table and do not touch them.

5. While you are watching you can begin sketching the cup and paper strips.

6. Use colored pencils to sketch what happens to the colors.

TRIAL 1—RECORD YOUR OBSERVATIONS

1. What colors showed up on the pieces of facial tissue and newsprint?

   COLOR OF LINE: _____

   COLORS ON NEWSPRINT: _____

   COLOR OF LINE: _____

   COLORS ON TISSUE: _____

2. What was the dominant color in this marker color? _____

3. What color was present that surprised you? _____

4. Is there any color marker that you think would have only 1 color?   **YES   NO**

   Which one would be most likely? _____

★ ★ ★ SAVE YOUR COLORED STRIPS. LET THEM DRY. ★ ★ ★

CAPILLARY ACTION

TRIAL 2—PREPARE NEW STRIPS AND CUPS

1. Choose a different marker. Do not use brown or black.

   What color marker did you choose? _____

2. Pour a little more than an inch of clean water into a clean cup.

3. Use the marker to make a wide mark at the 3" mark of each soft paper strip.

TRIAL 2—OBSERVE THE COLORS

1. Stand the colored end of each strip of soft paper in the water cup. The wide lines will be near the middle of the cups.

2. Bend the top of the newsprint and tissue over the lip of the cup. You don't want them to slide into the water. If necessary, use clear tape to hold them in place.

3. Record the time. _____ Plan to watch the reaction for at least 10 minutes.

4. Leave the cups and papers on the table and do not touch them.

5. While you are watching, you can begin sketching the cups and paper strips.

6. Use colored pencils sketch what happens to the colors.

TRIAL 2—RECORD YOUR OBSERVATIONS

1. What colors showed up on the pieces of facial tissue and newsprint?

   COLOR OF LINE: _____

   COLORS ON NEWSPRINT: _____

   COLOR OF LINE: _____

   COLORS ON TISSUE: _____

2. What was the dominant color in this marker color? _____

3. What color was present that surprised you? _____

★ ★ ★ SAVE YOUR COLORED STRIPS. LET THEM DRY. ★ ★ ★

CAPILLARY ACTION

Capillary action is the movement of a liquid along the surface of a solid. It is caused by the attraction of the liquid molecules to the solid molecules.

Markers are made using different pigments of color. You have observed the water soak the colors at the marker lines and carry the color up the soft papers. What colors do you think will show up when you test the brown marker?_____

TRIAL 3—PREPARE NEW STRIPS AND CUPS

1. Use a brown marker for your final trial. Use the brown marker to make a wide mark at the 3" line on the paper strips.

2. Pour a little more than an inch of clean water into a cup.

TRIAL 3—OBSERVE THE COLORS

1. Stand the colored end of each strip of soft paper in the water cup. The brown line should be at the middle of the cup.

2. Bend the top of the newsprint and tissue over the lip of the cup and use clear tape to hold them in place if you need to.

3. Record the time: _____ Plan to watch the reaction for at least 10 minutes.

4. Leave the cup and papers on the table and do not touch them.

5. While you are watching, you can begin sketching the cup and the paper strips.

6. Use colored pencils to sketch what happens to the colors.

TRIAL 3—RECORD YOUR OBSERVATIONS

1. What colors showed up on the pieces of facial tissue and newsprint?

    COLOR OF LINE: _____

    COLORS ON NEWSPRINT: _____

    COLOR OF LINE: _____

    COLORS ON TISSUE: _____

2. What was the dominant color in the brown marker? _____

3. What color was present that surprised you? _____

CAPILLARY ACTION

JOURNAL ENTRY

1. Explain how capillary action works. _____

_____

_____

_____

_____

2. What did you learn about the colored markers? _____

_____

_____

   Which color that you tested had the most colors? _____

   Which color that you tested had the fewest colors? _____

3. What was the most surprising information you learned today? _____

_____

_____

   Why? _____

_____

_____

4. What did you learn about the color brown? _____

_____

_____

_____

TEACHER NOTE: Answers may vary depending upon the maker of the markers.

SCIENTIFIC METHOD REVIEW—CAPILLARY ACTION

Share your journal entries, documents, and experiences with capillary action with your classmates during a class discussion led by your teacher.

CHALLENGE: TEST IT—USE THE SCIENTIFIC METHOD

Directions: Talk with your teacher. Decide on activities that can be done with the materials that are available.

ASK A QUESTION—WHAT DO YOU WANT TO TEST? Think of the materials you
have already used in the three activities. Was there another trial or test you wanted to do? Perhaps one of these ideas will be of interest:

- [ ] using the sun to dry one of the invisible inks
- [ ] mixing equal parts baking soda and water to make an invisible ink
- [ ] a variation of glop—adding more or less water, glue, or borax
- [ ] capillary action testing with the same color marker made by two different brands
- [ ] capillary action in celery or carnations
- [ ] other: _____

_____

RESEARCH

What research do you need to do before beginning?

_____

_____

_____

WHAT IS YOUR HYPOTHESIS?

Describe the experiment you are planning and what you think will happen.

_____

_____

_____

TEST WITH EXPERIMENTATION: Describe the reaction of each ingredient added for each
step of your experiment.

_____

_____

_____

REMINDER: No team should finish the lab work and report in less than 15 minutes.

NAME_____

CHALLENGE: TEST IT—USE THE SCIENTIFIC METHOD

ANALYZE: Did you succeed in proving your hypothesis?   **YES   NO**

Explain: _____

_____

_____

What was the final product or result of your experiment? _____

_____

_____

TROUBLESHOOT:

If you could do the experiment over, would you do anything differently?   **YES   NO**

If so, what and why? _____

_____

_____

COMMUNICATE RESULTS:

Do you believe your experiment was successful?   **YES   NO**

Explain: _____

What worked as you planned? _____

_____

What surprised you? _____

_____

Sketch or describe your results in the box below.

Common Core State Standards

Each lesson meets one or more of the following Common Core State Standards © Copyright 2010. National Governors Association Center for Best Practices and Council of Chief State School Officers. All rights reserved. For more information about the Common Core State Standards, go to *http://www.corestandards.org/* or *http://www.teachercreated.com/standards*.

Reading Informational Text Standards	Pages
Key Ideas and Details	
ELA.RI.3.1 Ask and answer questions to demonstrate understanding of a text, referring explicitly to the text as the basis for the answers.	24, 29, 30, 34, 37, 44–45, 47, 51, 54, 56–57, 63–64, 69, 73, 76, 80, 82–85, 90, 98, 104, 108, 115, 116, 117, 119, 125, 128, 131, 133, 135, 142, 148, 151, 156
ELA.RI.3.2 Determine the main idea of a text; recount the key details and explain how they support the main idea.	22–39, 42–59, 62–85, 88–110, 113–137, 140–158
ELA.RI.3.3 Describe the relationship between a series of historical events, scientific ideas or concepts, or steps in technical procedures in a text, using language that pertains to time, sequence, and cause/effect.	23–24, 25–29, 30–34, 35–37, 38–39, 43–44, 45–47, 48–51, 52–54, 55–57, 58–59, 63–64, 65–69, 70–73, 74–76, 77–80, 81–85, 89–90, 91–98, 99–104, 105–108, 109–110, 114–115, 118, 119, 120–125, 126–128, 129–131, 132–133, 134–135, 136–137, 142, 143–148, 149–151, 152–156, 157–158
Craft and Structure	
ELA.RI.3.4 Determine the meaning of general academic and domain-specific words and phrases in a text relevant to a grade 3 topic or subject area.	22, 42, 62, 88, 113, 140
Integration of Knowledge and Ideas	
ELA.RI.3.7 Use information gained from illustrations (e.g., maps, photographs) and the words in a text to demonstrate understanding of the text (e.g., where, when, why, and how key events occur).	22–39, 42–59, 62–85, 88–110, 113–137, 140–158
Range of Reading and Level of Text Complexity	
ELA.RI.3.10 By the end of the year, read and comprehend informational texts, including history/social studies, science, and technical texts, at the high end of the grades 2–3 text complexity band independently and proficiently.	22–39, 42–59, 62–85, 88–110, 113–137, 140–158

Writing Standards	Pages
Text Types and Purposes	
ELA.W.3.1 Write opinion pieces on topics or texts, supporting a point of view with reasons.	29, 34, 37, 51, 54, 63–64, 69, 76, 82–85, 131, 135, 141, 147–148, 151, 156
ELA.W.3.2 Write informative/explanatory texts to examine a topic and convey ideas and information clearly.	24, 29, 30, 34, 36–37, 38–39, 47, 51, 54, 57, 58–59, 63, 69, 73, 75–76, 79–80, 82–85, 89–90, 95, 98, 103–104, 108, 109–110, 116, 125, 128, 130–131, 133, 135, 136–137, 141, 147–148, 151, 156, 157–158
Research to Build and Present Knowledge	
ELA.W.3.7 Conduct short research projects that build knowledge about a topic.	22–39, 42–59, 62–85, 88–110, 113–137, 140–158
ELA.W.3.8 Recall information from experiences or gather information from print and digital sources; take brief notes on sources and sort evidence into provided categories.	22–39, 42–59, 62–85, 88–110, 113–137, 140–158

Speaking & Listening Standards	Pages
Presentation of Knowledge and Ideas	
ELA.SL.3.4 Report on a topic or text, tell a story, or recount an experience with appropriate facts and relevant, descriptive details, speaking clearly at an understandable pace.	29, 34, 37, 38–39, 47, 51, 54, 57, 58–59, 69, 73, 76, 80, 81–85, 98, 104, 108, 109–110, 125, 128, 131, 136–137, 148, 151, 156, 157–158

Next Generation Science Standards

3. Forces and Interactions	Pages
Students who demonstrate understanding can:	
3-PS2-1. Plan and conduct an investigation to provide evidence of the effects of balanced and unbalanced forces on the motion of an object.	
Unit 4—Air in Action	86–110
Unit 5—Simple Machines	111–137
3-PS2-2. Make observations and/or measurements of an object's motion to provide evidence that a pattern can be used to predict future motion.	
Unit 5—Simple Machines (Working with Levers)	120–125
Unit 5—Simple Machines (The Wedge and the Inclined Plane)	126–128
Unit 5—Simple Machines (The Wheel and Axle)	129–131
Unit 5—Simple Machines (The Screw)	132–133
Unit 5—Simple Machines (The Pulley)	134–135

3. Engineering Design	Pages
Students who demonstrate understanding can:	
3-5-ETS1-1. Define a simple design problem reflecting a need or a want that includes specified criteria for success and constraints on materials, time, or cost.	
Unit 1—Boats and Barges	20–39
Unit 2—Working with Sound	40–59
Unit 4—Air in Action	86–110
Unit 5—Simple Machines	111–137
3-5-ETS1-2. Generate and compare multiple possible solutions to a problem based on how well each is likely to meet the criteria and constraints of the problem.	
Unit 1—Boats and Barges	23–39
Unit 2—Working with Sound	43–59
Unit 3—Solutions, Mixtures, and Emulsions	65–85
Unit 4—Air in Action	89–110
Unit 5—Simple Machines	114–137
Unit 6—Classroom Chemistry	141–158
3-5-ETS1-3. Plan and carry out fair tests in which variables are controlled and failure points are considered to identify aspects of a model or prototype that can be improved.	
Unit 1—Boats and Barges	23–39
Unit 2—Working with Sound	43–59
Unit 3—Solutions, Mixtures, and Emulsions	65–85
Unit 4—Air in Action	89–110
Unit 5—Simple Machines	114–137
Unit 6—Classroom Chemistry	141–158